Improving Teacher Knowledge in K-12 Schooling

Xiaoxia A. Newton

Improving Teacher Knowledge in K-12 Schooling

Perspectives on STEM Learning

Xiaoxia A. Newton
College of Education
University of Massachusetts
Lowell, MA, USA

ISBN 978-3-030-10026-1   ISBN 978-3-319-71207-9   (eBook)
https://doi.org/10.1007/978-3-319-71207-9

To the four most important men in my life:
My late father, Wentai, who encouraged me to travel as far as
I could in order to pursue the best education available;
Brendan and Bryant, may you never lose your curiosity and creativity; and
Steve, for your fascination with my mathematics perspectives
that brought us together.

PREFACE

I was a postdoctoral scholar at Stanford when the National Math Panel (NMP), commissioned by the then President George W. Bush, came to give a public hearing. In his welcome speech to emphasize the important work the NMP members were doing, Stanford president at the time John Hennessey stated that roughly half of the Stanford undergraduates who declared as STEM (Science, Technology, Engineering and Mathematics) majors would eventually switch majors to a non-STEM field. I was startled upon hearing this statistic, but I did not quite understand at the time why Hennessey was focusing on attrition of STEM majors at a meeting about K-12 mathematics education. In the subsequent few years, I had the opportunity to investigate a group of undergraduate STEM majors' understanding of foundational algebra topics at another elite university. As reported in Chap. 4 of this book, I found that even these highly selective STEM majors do not necessarily possess an in-depth understanding of the basic algebraic topics they learned as K-12 students.

My study of undergraduate STEM majors complemented my earlier years' experiences leading a five-year evaluation of a large school district's mathematics reform initiative. I had the fortune to observe how teachers and students interact around mathematics in elementary, middle, and high school classrooms, to interview both teachers and mathematics coaches about their mathematical understanding of foundational arithmetic topics, and to observe various forms of in-service professional developments that were offered to teachers.

These research and evaluation opportunities have allowed me to come to a startling realization, the realization that mathematics teachers in the

USA have little systematic and explicit training of mathematical topics they are charged to teach. Their knowledge of K-12 topics comes mainly from their own K-12 learning experience. Too often this experience can be incoherent. They go on to college and take college mathematics that does not prepare them for teaching K-12 mathematics topics. They become classroom teachers and rely on textbooks that too often do not meet the mathematical standards in terms of mathematical coherence, logical thinking, mathematical reasoning and problem solving, precise definitions of mathematical concepts, and using definitions as a basis for making a valid mathematical argument (i.e., criteria that are acceptable among the mathematics community). Hence they pass on what they have learned as K-12 students themselves to their students.

Prior to my investigation of undergraduate STEM majors' mathematical understanding of foundational algebra topics, I assumed college mathematics courses would provide teachers with the necessary content knowledge for teaching K-12 students. Additionally, although I had noticed the content problem while studying the K-12 classroom mathematics teaching and learning, I was not aware of the problems with K-12 mathematics textbooks in their presentation of mathematical content.

To a great extent, my assumptions are not unique. In July 2014, the New York Times Magazine published an article titled "Why do Americans stink at math?" The article was written by Elizabeth Green, journalist and author of New York Times Bestseller, *Building a Better Teacher*. Green argued that Americans are terrible at mathematics because mathematics teaching is bad. Therefore, she argued that improving teaching would raise Americans' mathematics performance. Green's argument rests on a couple of assumptions that many, if not most of us, take for granted.

The first assumption is that there is nothing wrong with the mathematical content encoded in the K-12 textbooks, which forms the basis of the mathematics curriculum and is the primary source of mathematical knowledge on K-12 mathematics topics for both students and their teachers. The second assumption is that the mathematical content knowledge teachers gained through their college mathematics courses will help them to teach K-12 mathematical content.

Well, it turns out that both of these two widely held assumptions are mistaken. This book shows why these assumptions are incorrect. I will describe how several key components of the mathematics education system in the USA work against the goal of improving students' mathematical learning by failing to provide their teachers with opportunities to learn the mathematics they are charged to teach. These components consist of teachers' own learning experiences as students in K-12 classrooms, their undergraduate or graduate training in mathematics, and their in-service professional development training. These components coincide with three critical stages where teachers of mathematics gain mathematical knowledge to teach, namely, as K-12 learners themselves, as prospective teachers, and as in-service teachers.

To address the problem at its root, I argue that unless we improve each component so that the system will work and recognize the importance of teaching future mathematics teachers explicitly and rigorously the topics they are expected to teach, teachers will continue to recycle a body of fragmented, incoherent, and incomprehensible mathematical knowledge to their students, because these are the only types of mathematical knowledge they have at their disposal, both in terms of what they themselves have learned as K-12 students and in terms of the mathematical resources available to them, including the textbooks they rely on to teach as mathematics teachers.

Lowell, MA, USA   Xiaoxia A. Newton

ACKNOWLEDGEMENT

I thank my doctoral advisor, Noreen (Rennie) Webb, for her mentorship and support and for being a role model instilling in me the value of a work-life balance. As someone in her twenties arriving in the USA with little cultural knowledge but many fears of living and studying in a country thousands-of-miles away from home, I feel fortunate to have met Reenie as the first American teacher and friend.

I also thank all professors and colleagues whom I have met over the years during my academic and professional career, especially Mike Seltzer, Marvin Alkin, Mike Rose, Linda Darling-Hammond, Denis Phillips, Sophia Rabe-Hesketh, Mark Wilson, Bruce Fuller, Marcia Linn, Lisa Garcia Bedolla, Janelle Scott, Tina Trujillo, Rick Mintrop, and Ann Foley. I would like to thank Mike Seltzer in particular, whose thoughtful approach to investigating educational problems through creative use of research methodology sets up a standard that I look up to.

I want to express my sincere gratitude to Professor Hung-Hsi Wu, a mathematician whose writings on mathematics education and whose efforts at improving K-12 mathematics teachers' content knowledge through summer professional development institutes over the past two decades have crystalized my own thinking on the "content problem" I have observed that permeates classroom mathematics teaching and learning.

I thank my doctoral advisees whom I worked with, in particular, Dr. Rebecca Poon who worked as a graduate student researcher on one of my research projects that formed the basis of Chaps. 4 and 6 of this book.

I also thank my parents, who provided me with a blessed childhood and supported me financially to pursue the best education possible in China. Whenever I think of selfless love, I think of my parents and look up to them as I am raising my own children. I also thank my extended family in America. Their warmth alleviates the homesickness I feel whenever I miss my family and relatives in China.

Last but not least, I want to thank my husband, Steve, for his unwavering support, companionship, and intellectual enthusiasm. My professional accomplishment means so much more because of you and our little boys.

This book would not have been possible without these wonderful people and many others I have met along the way. I thank them from the bottom of my heart.

CONTENTS

LIST OF FIGURES

LIST OF TABLES

CHAPTER 1

Introduction

When I was first tasked to take charge of a large-scale mathematics evaluation during the heyday of No Child Left Behind (NCLB), one of my friends sent me the following message, just to make me chuckle:

Subject: The History of Teaching Math [in the USA]

Teaching Math in 1950:
A logger sells a truckload of lumber for $100.
His cost of production is 4/5 of the price.
What is his profit?

Teaching Math in 1960:
A logger sells a truckload of lumber for $100.
His cost of production is 4/5 of the price, or $80.
What is his profit?

Teaching Math in 1970:
A logger exchanges a set "L" of lumber for a set "M" of money.
The cardinality of set "M" is 100. Each element is worth one dollar.
Make 100 dots representing the elements of the set "M."
The set "C", the cost of production, contains 20 fewer points than set "M."
Represent the set "C" as a subset of set "M" and answer the following question:
What is the cardinality of the set "P" of profits?

© The Author(s) 2018
X. A. Newton, *Improving Teacher Knowledge in K-12 Schooling*,
https://doi.org/10.1007/978-3-319-71207-9_1

1

Teaching Math in 1980:
A logger sells a truckload of lumber for $100.
His cost of production is $80 and his profit is $20.
Your assignment: Underline the number 20.

Teaching Math in 1990:
By cutting down beautiful forest trees, the logger makes $20.
What do you think of this way of making a living?
Topic for class participation after answering the question:
How did the forest birds and squirrels feel as the logger cut down the trees?
There are no wrong answers.

Teaching Match in 2000:
A logger sells a truckload of lumber for $100.
His cost of production is $120.
How does Arthur Andersen determine that his profit margin is $60?

Despite the cynicism contained in this portrait of the history of teaching mathematics in the USA, it is a fact that improving K-12 students' opportunities to learn and performance in mathematics and science has been of major concern for several decades (National Council of Teachers of Mathematics 2000; National Mathematics Advisory Panel 2008; National Research Council 2001). Despite waves of education reforms on K-12 mathematics and science teaching and learning, American students' performance in these subjects remains lackluster when compared to their international peers (Loveless 2013; National Center for Education Statistics 2004; Programme for International Student Assessment 2003). Scholars from different disciplines and with different perspectives have offered a variety of reasons for why this is so. These explanations range from language (e.g., Fuson and Kwon 1991), social beliefs and cultural values (e.g., Chazan 2000; Stevenson et al. 1993), parental involvement (e.g., Stevenson and Stigler 1992), teaching and learning behaviors (e.g., Hiebert et al. 2005; Stevenson et al. 1986; Stevenson and Stigler 1992; Stigler and Hiebert 1999, 2009), to curriculum and textbooks (e.g., Cai et al. 2002; Schmidt et al. 1997). But one area that remains relatively underexplored and underemphasized is teachers' lack of systematic opportunities to study and develop in-depth mathematical content understanding of topics that they are charged to teach at K-12 levels (Shulman 1986).

Though research on mathematics education has done a good job of documenting teachers' lack of mathematical understanding and its impact on student learning (e.g., Ball 1990, 1993, 2000; Ball et al. 2005; Ball and Rowan 2004; Cohen and Ball 2001; Hill and Ball 2004), we know little about where the deficiency of mathematical understanding came from, or what might be the possible remedies besides the typical argument for improving the pedagogy (e.g., Green 2015; Lampert 2001).

This book shows how several key components of the mathematics education system in the USA work against the goal of improving students' mathematics learning by failing to provide their teachers with opportunities to learn the mathematics they are charged to teach. These components consist of classroom mathematics learning experiences, undergraduate or graduate training, and in-service professional development. These components coincide with three critical stages where teachers of mathematics gain mathematical knowledge to teach: namely, as K-12 learners themselves, as prospective teachers, and as in-service teachers. This book argues that unless we recognize the importance of teaching future mathematics teachers explicitly and rigorously the topics they are expected to teach, teachers will continue to recycle a body of incoherent and incomprehensible mathematical knowledge to their students, because these are the only types of mathematical knowledge they have at their disposal, both in terms of what they themselves have learned as K-12 students and in terms of the mathematical resources available to them, including the textbooks they have to teach with as mathematics teachers.

In the sections that follow, I will describe when I first noticed the problem with mathematical content understanding through an example of classroom mathematics teaching and learning. My observations have led me to a research path investigating both students' and teachers' opportunities to learn mathematics. This research path is the basis for this book. The chapter ends with an overview of the subsequent chapters.

HOW DID I BECOME INTERESTED IN STUDYING MATHEMATICAL CONTENT UNDERSTANDING?

The following episode describes one elementary teacher who was reviewing and teaching her 2nd graders the concept of probability through experiment. She first asked one student to read the definition of probability and then did the experiment to show what it meant.

T[1] Yesterday, we used cubes. Today we are going to use something different. Here is a card, one side is red and one side is blue. I'm going to drop the card on the floor 10 times. John, read the definition of probability.

John [reads the definition]

T   What is the probability that it will end up more red or more blue?

John [no response]

T   We are going to flip it 10 times to see what comes up. I need a helper, Amanda, to check off on the chart whether it comes up blue or red, the probability or how likely something will happen. Anita, I'd like you to call it when it drops on the floor.

The teacher dropped the card 10 times and the results were as follows:

	1	2	3	4	5	6	7	8	9	10
Blue	×	×	×	×	×	×				
Red							×	×	×	×

T   How many times did it land on blue?

Students [counted] 6

T   How many times did it land on red?

Students [counted] 4

T   Did it end up in a tie?

Students No.

T   Close to a tie?

Students Yes.

T   It's pretty close to being even.

In fact, this teacher was following the textbook. Although the textbook's idea of teaching the concept of probability through experiment was a good one, whether students were able to understand the concept or not ultimately depends on the teacher's understanding of the concept, particularly when students were confused by the seemingly inconsistent experiment results and what they had learned about the concept of probability, as the following interaction shows:

T   Let's try a different object. The next object is a penny. Steve, how many sides to a coin?

Steve   2

T   How many sides are heads?

Steve   1

T   How many sides are tails?

Steve   1

T   Is there a greater chance for it to be heads, tails or equal?

John   Equal, because there are 2 sides.

T   What about this? [She refers to the experiment results of the card chart.] Why?

David   Because there are 2 sides, 1 heads and 1 tails

T   Does anyone think any differently?

Brandi   Heads more.

T   Why? Raise hands if you agree.
      [Some students did]

T   Raise your hands if you think it will land on tails.
      [Some students did]

In this example, most of the interactions proceeded well—the teacher asked a few scaffolding questions before turning to the first main question, that is, "Is there a greater chance for it to be heads, tails or equal" if she were to drop the coin. John answered the question correctly by saying that it would be "equal", but he did not just stop by offering only an answer. John also explained that the reason why he thought the answer was equal was "because there are two sides [to a coin]." The teacher challenged John by asking "what about this?" and "why?" referring to the result from the experiment they did earlier in the lesson.

The teacher did an excellent job here by pushing John to think further. In the experiment they did earlier, a card with two sides (blue and red) was dropped 10 times. The result for the card to be blue and red turned out to be 6 and 4, respectively. A coin has two sides (heads and tails), just as a card with two sides. The card with two sides did not come out even when dropped 10 times. The teacher was asking whether the chance of the coin having unequal numbers of heads and tails when it is dropped a few times is possible. John did not follow up the teacher's challenge

with an answer, but David did, although his answer was irrelevant—
"Because there are 2 sides, 1 heads and 1 tails." The teacher did not point
out the irrelevance of David's answer; instead she asked, "Does anyone think
any differently?" Brandi realized that the chance of the card to be equally
blue and red was not supported by the result of their experiment. She then
answered, "Heads more." It was unclear why she chose heads as if it were the
blue side of the card used in the earlier experiment, but the important
thing is that she probably had made the connection that if the blue and
red did not turn out to be equal, heads and tails would probably not
turn out to be equal. The teacher asked, "Why?" but then forced a yes/
no choice from the students by asking them to raise hands. This was
where the teacher could have moved the interaction along the direction
of discovering reasoning instead of pursuing a correct answer. If the
teacher had probed further using the why questions instead of asking
the students to raise hands if they agreed or disagreed, they would have
had an opportunity to discuss, if not discover, why an object with two
sides (e.g., the card with blue and red, a coin with heads and tails) did
not come out equal when dropped a few times.

The students had been told in previous lessons that the chance should
be equal, given that this was their third lesson on the concept of probability. The teacher could be of great help in this situation. For instance, after
further probing, if the students still could not explain why, the teacher
could have helped them by pointing out that the card was dropped only
10 times. If they were to drop the card an infinite number of times, the
proportions for the card to be blue and red would approach the same
amount. And when we talk about the probability of something being
equal, we are referring to infinity or in the long run (a thought experiment).
Ten times is not infinity. This rationale would have helped the students to
explain the discrepancy between what they learned and what they saw
from the experiment and therefore better understand the concept of probability. However, the discussion was very brief and the teacher did not
pursue it further in the direction of helping students to conceptually
understand the concept of probability. In doing so, the teacher did not
demonstrate her fundamental understanding of the concept of probability,
which, in turn, limited her ability to clarify the students' confusion.

The example described above is just one of the thousands of classroom
mathematics teaching and learning lesson data my research team collected

across elementary, middle, and high schools over a period of five years. These lesson observations reveal a common pattern in US mathematics lessons that has important implications for how mathematics is learned: a discourse norm[2] that systematically cuts mathematical discussion short of the point of explicit discussion of mathematical concepts. This observation led me on a research path to examine the mathematics embedded in lessons across classrooms at all levels of schools (Chap. 2) and eventually to investigate system actors' (i.e., teachers and mathematics coaches) understanding of basic mathematical ideas (Chap. 3) and their opportunities to learn mathematics as pre-service (Chap. 4) and in-service teachers (Chap. 5).

SWIMMING UPSTREAM: MY RESEARCH PATH

Swimming upstream is a nice way to capture my research path in terms of investigating systematically how the mathematics education system works in the USA. Figure. 1.1 displays the journey I traveled researching several key components of the mathematics education system, from examining

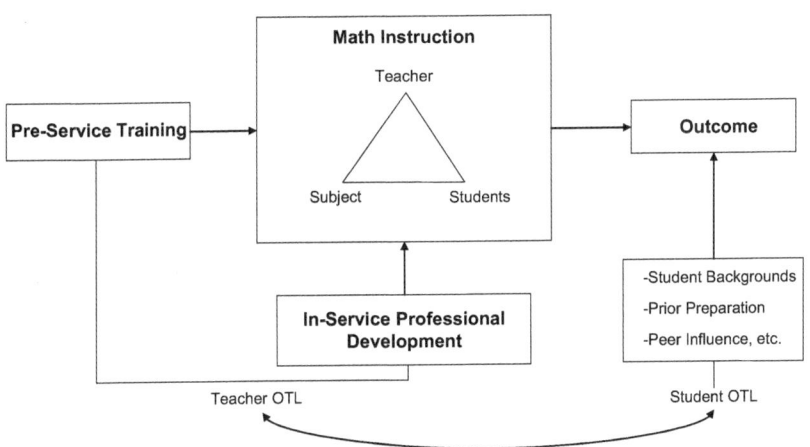

Fig. 1.1   Research path: swimming upstream (*OTL*: opportunities to learn)

patterns and predictors of student outcomes in mathematics (i.e., the downstream), to unpacking what happens when teachers and students come together to interact around mathematics in day-to-day classroom instruction, and examining teachers' opportunities to learn (OTL) and deepen their mathematical content understanding through various professional development activities (i.e., the mid-stream), and finally to learning how teachers are trained to teach mathematics through pre-service education (i.e., the upstream).

More specifically, my early work focused on gender differences in mathematics growth during middle and high school and college STEM (Science, Technology, Engineering and Mathematics) participation, utilizing data from large-scale quantitative survey projects sponsored by the National Science Foundation (NSF). My analyses showed that the disparity in students' mathematics achievement later in life (e.g., college degree attainment in STEM) could be traced back to as early as middle school, or possibly even earlier. Opportunities to take progressively more advanced mathematics courses throughout secondary school years appeared to be one of the key factors predicting students' future mathematics attainment (Ai 2002; Newton 2010; Newton et al. 2011).

Quantitative analysis of large-scale data led me to wonder what day-to-day classroom instruction might look like in the USA and what implications classroom instruction may have for students' mathematical learning. My evaluation experience as the project director of a five-year longitudinal evaluation of the District Mathematics Plan (DMP) in one of the largest urban school districts allowed me the opportunity to examine systematically classroom mathematics instruction and the kinds of in-service professional development opportunities that teachers receive. My analysis of classroom mathematics teaching and learning reveals a common pattern in US mathematics lessons that also has important implications for how mathematics is learned: a discourse norm that systematically cuts mathematical discussion short of the point of explicit discussion of mathematical concepts. This pattern is observable not in the back and forth between teachers and students but in lessons seen as a whole. Over time, because advanced mathematics knowledge builds on earlier understanding, students encounter new topics ill-prepared to understand them.

In an attempt to understand the pattern of mathematics classroom instruction, I subsequently investigated teachers' and mathematics coaches' mathematical understanding of foundational topics and also examined teachers' opportunities to learn through various in-service professional development activities. Consistent with the discourse norm of mathematics instruction, I found that teachers and mathematics coaches focus on algorithms instead of mathematical understanding. Though teachers had opportunities to participate in various professional development activities such as workshops or peer coaching, these training activities focus on what to do and rarely on understanding the mathematical concepts so as to make sense of why the algorithm works.

My work in teacher pre-service training is a natural extension of my intellectual interests, from understanding teachers' opportunities to learn as teachers, to asking the questions about how teachers are trained to teach. This is another important component of the system, connecting teachers' preparation with their ability to engage students to learn mathematics. It is typically assumed that majoring in a subject area is equivalent to having solid content knowledge for teaching that subject at the K-12 level (Ball 1990). My research examining the nature of mathematical understanding of three foundational early algebra topics among a group of undergraduate STEM majors showed that many of the STEM majors in our study sample did not possess deep understanding of the three topics we investigated. This suggests that even though these STEM majors might be strong in their disciplinary knowledge, they do not necessarily have the depth of understanding of K-12 topics in order to teach at that level (Newton and Poon 2015a, b).

Putting It All Together: This Book

This book is a synthesis of work I have done along my intellectual journey of trying to understand how the mathematics education system works in the USA. This journey has led me to the insight that key components of the mathematics education system in the USA work against the goal of improving students' mathematical outcomes by failing to provide teachers of mathematics with an explicit and rigorous training of mathematical topics that they are charged to teach. In this book, I demonstrate why this is the case and argue for higher education institutions to step up in order to address the issue of mathematics teachers' content preparation.

In Chap. 2, extensive qualitative content analyses of classroom mathematics teaching and learning show how the concept of place value in grades 2, 4, 8, and 10 were taught and the impact on students' learning of the concept and its application in different mathematical contexts. The analyses documented how teachers followed a discourse norm that focused on procedural knowledge and failed to create opportunities for students to learn mathematical concepts. Students were unable to construct mathematically valid arguments even in honors classes in the upper grades. The chapter also shows that students at these upper grades did not have a solid grasp of the concept of place value that should have been addressed beginning in early grades.

Chapter 3 presents data on teachers' and mathematics coaches' understanding of two mathematical topics: subtraction with regrouping and multi-digit multiplication. These two topics involve understanding of the concept of place value and represent two standard topics in elementary mathematics. These two topics are purposely chosen because they provide us with a glimpse of educators' understanding of a basic mathematical concept (i.e., place value) and its application in these two common mathematical topics. The central purpose of the chapter is to emphasize the fact that as simple as these two mathematical topics may seem to be on the surface, the depth of understanding that is required in order to teach effectively (or teach well) is not as simple as we may think.

Chapter 4 describes a group of undergraduate STEM majors' understanding of slope as defined by the Common Core Mathematics Standards (CCMS). Common Core Mathematics Standards is a major effort at revamping US K-12 mathematics education in order to improve American students' mathematical performance and international competitiveness. To ensure the successful implementation of CCMS, there have been calls for both recruiting from those with the strongest quantitative backgrounds (e.g., STEM majors) and offering rigorous mathematics training in teacher preparation. Missing from the literature are questions about whether STEM majors, who arguably represent the strongest candidates for the teaching force, have the depth of content understanding in order to teach mathematical topics at the rigorous level that CCMS expects, and whether future mathematics teachers need the opportunities to learn rigorously the K-12 mathematical topics they are expected to teach further down the road. This chapter addresses the knowledge gap in these two areas through investigating the understanding of the concept of slope among a group STEM majors who were enrolled in an undergraduate experimental teacher preparation program. The investigation of STEM majors' understanding of a foundational algebra concept provides a window through which to address the issue of content training of mathematics teachers in general.

Chapter 5 examines teachers' opportunities (or lack of) to learn mathematics through various in-service professional development activities and instructional tools intended to provide support to teachers. The investigation into teachers' and mathematics coaches' mathematical content understanding suggests that teachers must develop a deep conceptual understanding of mathematics. Teachers' opportunities to learn (OTL) will influence teachers' ability to adopt new beliefs and practices. These opportunities to learn will come mainly through their participation in various professional development activities. In a similar manner, those who are in a position to provide professional development for teachers (e.g., mathematics coaches) also need to possess a profound understanding of mathematics (Ma 1999, 2010).

Chapter 6 offers a perspective on what conceptual understanding means when we focus on a particular mathematical topic or concept and what differentiates conceptual understanding from fragile understanding. The chapter answers these questions through illustrating what in-depth understanding of mathematical topics might look like. I describe two major criteria and a framework that outlines central characteristics exemplified in mathematical conceptual understanding and illustrate how these characteristics manifest themselves in specific topics I have conducted research on. This chapter is foundational in terms of setting a benchmark against the kinds of understanding that teachers are exposed to which can be characterized as fragmented, incoherent, and superficial.

Chapter 7 focuses on several contextual factors that shape teachers' and students' opportunities to learn mathematics. This chapter is important because what we observe in classroom teaching and learning and what we see in students' performance on various accountability measures such as high-stakes, large-scale, standardized tests are products of many things. Among these many things are how teachers themselves learned the subject matter, how they were trained to be teachers during their credentialing process, and how they were trained and supported once they enter the teaching force. Consequently, in presenting what we have observed in the way that teachers engage their students about mathematics, we must also be attentive to some of the broader contextual issues in order to put the findings in a proper perspective. Among these contextual factors are the US cultural assumptions and beliefs about mathematics teaching and learning, the US K-12 school system and the challenges involved in changing core practice, and the impact of the No Child Left Behind (NCLB) Act and its successor Every Student Succeeds Act (ESSA) which are the backbone of the Federal accountability system. These contextual factors largely define the challenges involved in improving the teaching and learning conditions for mathematics. Finally, higher education institutions need to step up their effort at addressing future mathematics teachers' content training issues.

NOTES

1. T: teacher; all names are pseudonyms.
2. I use this term (discourse norm) to describe interactively the following four aspects of a lesson involving mathematics teaching and learning: (1) portrait of mathematics knowledge; (2) role of teachers; (3) role of students; and (4) conversations about mathematics.

REFERENCES

Ai, X. (2002). Gender differences in growth in mathematics achievement: Three-level longitudinal and multilevel analyses of individual, home, and school influences. *Mathematical Thinking and Learning, 4*(1), 1–22.

Ball, D. L. (1990). The mathematical understanding that prospective teachers bring to teacher education. *Elementary School Journal, 90,* 449–466.

Ball, D. (1993). With an eye of the mathematical horizon: Dilemmas of teaching elementary school mathematics. *Elementary School Journal, 93*(4), 373–397.

Ball, D. (2000). Bridging practices: Intertwining content and pedagogy in teaching and learning to teach. *Journal of Teacher Education, 51*(3), 241–247.

Ball, D. L., & Rowan, B. (2004). Introduction: Measuring instruction. *Elementary School Journal, 105*(1), 3–10.

Ball, D. L., Hill, H. C., & Bass, H. (2005). Knowing mathematics for teaching: Who knows mathematics well enough to teach third grade, and how can we decide? *American Educator, 29*(1), 14–17, 20–22, 43–46.

Cai, J., Lo, J. J., & Watanabe, T. (2002). Intended treatment of arithmetic average in U.S. and Asia school mathematics textbooks. *School Science and Mathematics, 102*(8), 1–13.

Chazan, D. (2000). *Beyond formulas in mathematics and teaching: Dynamics of the high school algebra classroom.* New York: Teacher College Press.

Cohen, D. K., & Ball, D. L. (2001). Making change: Introduction and its improvement. *Phi Delta Kappan, 83*(1), 73–77.

Fuson, K., & Kwon, Y. (1991). Chinese-based regular and European irregular systems of number words: The disadvantages for English-speaking children. In K. Durkin & B. Shire (Eds.), *Language in mathematics education: Research and practice* (pp. 211–226). Milton Keynes: Open University Press.

Green, E. (2015). *Building a better teacher: How teaching works (and how to teach it to everyone)*. New York: W.W. Norton & Company, Inc.

Hiebert, J., Stigler, J., Jacobs, J., Givvin, K., Garnier, H., Smith, M., Hollingsworth, H., Manaster, A., Wearne, D., & Gallimore, R. (2005). Mathematics teaching in the United States today (and tomorrow): Results from the TIMSS 1999 video study. *Educational Evaluation and Policy Analysis, 27*(2), 111–112.

Hill, H., & Ball, D. (2004). Learning mathematics for teaching: Results from California's mathematics professional development institutes. *Journal for Research in Mathematics Education, 35*(5), 330–351.

Lampert, M. (2001). *Teaching problems and the problems of teaching*. New Haven: Yale University Press.

Loveless, T. (2013). The 2013 Brown Center Report on American Education: How well are American students learning? With sections on the latest international tests, tracking and ability grouping, and advanced math in 8th grade. Accessible at: http://www.brookings.edu/~/media/research/files/reports/2013/03/18-brown-center-loveless/2013-brown-center-report-web.pdf

Ma, L. (1999). *Knowing and teaching elementary mathematics: Teachers' understanding of fundamental mathematics in China and the United States*. Mahwah: Lawrence Erlbaum Associates.

Ma, L. (2010). *Knowing and teaching elementary mathematics: Teachers' understanding of fundamental mathematics in China and the United States* (2nd ed.). New York: Routledge.

National Center for Education Statistics. (2004). *Highlights from the trends in international mathematics and science study (TIMSS) 2003*. Washington, DC: Author.

National Council of Teachers of Mathematics. (2000). *Principles and standards for school mathematics*. Reston: Author.

National Mathematics Advisory Panel. (2008). *Foundations for success: The final report of the National Mathematics Advisory Panel*, U.S. Department of Education, Washington, DC.

National Research Council. (2001). Adding it up: Helping children learn mathematics. In J. Kilpatrick, J. Swafford, & B. Findell (Eds.), *Mathematics learning study committee, center for education, division of behavior and social sciences, and education*. Washington, DC: National Academies Press.

Newton, X. (2010). End of high school mathematics attainment: How did students get there? *Teachers College Record, 112*(4), 1064–1095.

Newton, X., & Poon, R. (2015a). Mathematical content understanding for teaching: A study of undergraduate STEM majors. *Creative Education, 6*(10), 998–1031. https://doi.org/10.4236/ce.2015.610101.

Newton, X., & Poon, R. (2015b). Pre-service STEM majors' understanding of slope according to Common Core Mathematics Standards: An exploratory study. *Global Journal of Human Social Science Research, 15*(7), 27–42.

Newton, X., Torres, D., & Rivero, R. (2011). Making the connection: Timing of taking algebra and future college STEM participation. *Journal of Women and Minorities in Science and Engineering, 17*(2), 129–146.

Programme for International Student Assessment. (2003). *First results from PISA 2003.* Paris: Author.

Schmidt, W. H., McKnight, C. C., & Raizens, S. A. (1997). *A splinted vision: An investigation of U.S. science and mathematics education.* Boston: Kluwer.

Shulman, L. (1986). Those who understand: Knowledge growth in teaching. *Educational Researcher, 15*, 4–14.

Stevenson, H. W., & Stigler, J. W. (1992). *The learning gap: Why our schools are failing and what we can learn from Japanese and Chinese education?* New York: Summit Books.

Stevenson, H. W., Stigler, J. W., & Lee, S. Y. (1986). Achievement in mathematics. In H. W. Stevenson, H. Azuma, & K. Hakuta (Eds.), *Children development and education in Japan* (pp. 201–218). New York: Freeman.

Stevenson, H. W., Chen, C., & Lee, S. Y. (1993). Mathematics achievement of Chinese, Japanese, and American children: Ten years later. *Science, 259*(1), 53–58.

Stigler, J., & Hiebert, J. (1999). *The teaching gap: Best ideas from the world's teachers for improving education in the classroom.* New York: Free Press.

Stigler, J., & Hiebert, J. (2009). *The teaching gap: Best ideas from the world's teachers for improving education in the classroom (updated).* New York: Free Press.

CHAPTER 2

K-12 Mathematical Learning Experiences

This chapter presents extensive qualitative content analysis based on observations of classroom mathematics teaching and learning, and shows how the concept of place value in grades 2, 4, 8, and 10 are taught and the impact on students' learning of the concept and its application in different mathematical contexts. The analyses document how teachers follow a discourse norm focused on procedural knowledge and how this norm fails to allow for opportunities to learn mathematical concepts. Students were unable to construct mathematically valid arguments even in honors classes in the upper grades. The analysis also shows that students at these upper grades did not have a solid grasp of the concept of place value that should have been addressed beginning in early grades.

Following the Teaching of a Basic Mathematics Idea Across the Elementary, Middle, and High School Classrooms

Figure 2.1 displays five classroom cases described in this chapter.

As shown in Fig. 2.1, the five classroom cases included two 2nd grade classes, one 4th grade class, one 8th grade Algebra 1 class, and one Honors Algebra 2 class that consisted of mostly 10th grade students. The five classes, each of which were observed on three different occasions (i.e., three lessons per class), were purposefully selected because, at the

© The Author(s) 2018   15
X. A. Newton, *Improving Teacher Knowledge in K-12 Schooling*,
https://doi.org/10.1007/978-3-319-71207-9_2

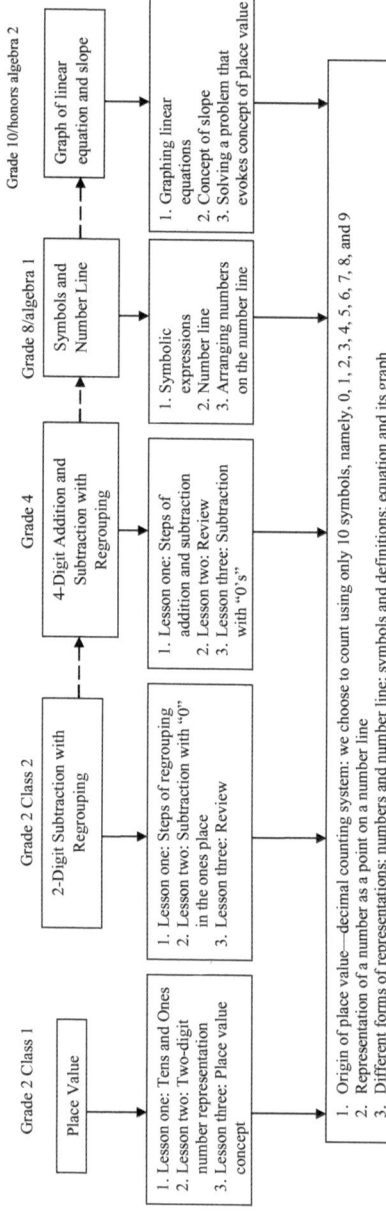

Fig. 2.1 Approximate representation of mathematics coherence

time of observations, students in these classes were learning a common mathematical concept (i.e., place value) in different contexts. These cases allow us to perceive a longitudinal story through a cross-sectional sample. The analysis traces classrooms focused on the concept of place value and related concepts across multiple grades, and shows how the limited conceptual understanding observable in students at higher grades (middle and high) reflects how the concept is introduced in elementary grades.

First 2nd Grade Class: Tens and Ones: Are Students Provided Opportunities to Learn the Decimal Counting System and the Concept of Place Value?

The first case consists of a 2nd grade math class engaged in three consecutive lessons designed to elucidate the concept of place value. The goal of the first lesson, as described by the teacher, was for students to understand "what a ten is. That a ten is made up ten ones." Here is how the lesson began.

(1) T^1: Are we ready for math? We are moving on today with bigger numbers.

Tens are bigger numbers. With bigger numbers, it's a lot easier to count by ten.

[T spills a handful of colored, plastic, counting disks on the screen of the overhead projector.]

(2) T: How do I find out how many [counters] I have?

(3) Ss: Don't know.

(4) T: Why?

(5) Ss: They are all stuck together.

(6) T: Would it be easier if I had one group of ten? Each of these is called a one. How many counters in the group?

[T counts out 10.]

(7) T: One group of ten is equal to ten ones.

[T makes another group of 10.]

(8) T: How many groups of ten do I have?

(9) Ss: 2.

(10) T: Here I have ten ones and here I have ten ones. How many groups is that?

(11) Ss: 2.

(12) T: How many are in these two groups?

(13) GH: 20.
(14) T: How many ones are in these two groups?
(15) Ss: 20 ones.
    [T makes a third group of ten.]
(16) T: I have ten ones plus ten ones plus ten ones. How many is that?
(17) BH: 30.
(18) T: I'm going to make another group. [Counting out the rest] Do I have enough? No. I only have seven. Let's count our tens.
(19) T/Ss: 10, 20, 30.
(20) T: So, I have 30 and 7. My number is 37.

As this interaction episode shows, the concept of tens and ones was stated to students as a fact. Once the rule that 1 ten equals 10 ones was established, the teacher led the class to practice repeatedly that 1 ten equals 10 ones, that 10 ones equal 1 ten, that 2 tens equal 20 ones, that 20 ones equal 2 tens, and so on. In fact, for the remainder of the class (58 minutes long), all the class did was to practice the same drill over and over again. At the end of the class, the teacher tried to summarize what they learned by asking:

(21) T: When you look at your math words, which ones did we learn today?
(22) Desiree: 100.
(23) Patrick: tens.
(24) Anas: tens and ones.
(25) T: We talked about tens and groups of ones. At home there's an activity to do with your family. Put the letter under your box to take home today.

Although the teacher's attempt to help the students remember the concept they just learned at the end of the lesson was well intended, the teacher did not appear to achieve her stated purpose (i.e., to understand what a ten is). As shown by the instructional episodes, the students were never given the opportunity to understand the relationship between tens and ones, other than being given the fact that 1 ten equals 10 ones and 10 ones make 1 ten. It is not surprising, therefore, that students might have got only fragmented mathematical ideas. As evidenced by students' responses, Desiree gave an irrelevant number (100), while Patrick gave part of the number (tens). Although Anas was able to articulate that they learned tens and ones, she did not state the relationship between the two, at least in the form that was taught (i.e., 1 ten equals 10 ones and 10 ones make 1 ten). The teacher's intention was for students to know this fact, therefore, following Ana's response, the teacher could have at least given some feedback such as "We talked about tens and ones and groups of tens. We have learned that 10 ones make 1 ten, whereas 1 ten equals 10 ones."

Of course, teaching students the mere fact that a ten is made up of 10 ones, or 10 ones make 1 ten without placing such a relationship in the context of how numbers are composed in the decimal system and its application in basic mathematical operations (e.g., subtraction with regrouping or addition with carrying) will not help students understand why they need to learn 1 ten is made up of 10 ones, or 10 ones make 1 ten. In fact, when we tell students that 1 ten is made up of 10 ones and that 10 ones make 1 ten, we have touched upon a fundamental concept of how numbers are composed in the decimal system (i.e., how to count in the Hindu-Arabic numeral system).

From a mathematical perspective, in the Hindu-Arabic numeral system (i.e., decimal system), we use ten (10) symbols to count, i.e., from 0 to 9. These symbols are referred to as digits and putting these digits in different places or positions (from right to left) makes it possible to write down all possible counting numbers (Wu 2011, sections 1.1 and 1.2). For instance, if we are allowed one place, using the ten symbols, we could count from 0 to 9 as follows:

0   1   2   3   4   5   6   7   8   9

But suppose we are allowed two places, then we could recycle the ten symbols (0–9) and continue our counting as follows:

00   01   02   03   04   05   06   07   08   09
10   11   12   13   14   15   16   17   18   19
20   21   22   23   24   25   26   27   28   29
...
90   91   92   93   94   95   96   97   98   99

These will be the numbers we get if we are restricted to two places and we call these numbers two-digit numbers. Why should we restrict ourselves to two places? Of course, we do not and therefore we go to three places and recycle the ten symbols again. This process explains why it takes 10 steps to go from 0 to 10, 10 to 20, 20 to 30, etc. And it explains why going from one place to two places (or two places to three places) is ten times.

Consequently, in the interactional episode shown in this 2nd grade class, a simple question such as "What happens to the number as we go from 9 to 10?" could have led the students into a rich discovery process of the meaning of place value rather than the mathematically incomplete notion that one 10 equals ten 1's. Otherwise, students may learn all the mathematical facts and/or procedures, but may never understand the underlying concepts.

During the observation of the second lesson of the same class, the teacher indicated that the focus of the lesson was to "represent a number with a model. Say a number in three different ways." At the beginning of the lesson, the teacher briefly reviewed with the class that 10 ones equal 1 ten and 1 ten equals 10 ones. The teacher then began the topic of the day.

(26) T: Help me make a model for the number 25. [T holds up two rods. Students count with the teacher.]
(27) T/Ss: 10, 20.
(28) T: That's 2 tens. That's my model for 20. But I need 5 more. Do I need 5 tens or 5 ones?
(29) Ss: Ones.
(30) T/Ss: 1, 2, 3, 4, 5 [count out 5 ones].
(31) T: This is my model for 25 using my base 10 blocks.
     [T repeats the same procedure for the number 43.]

After demonstrating how to model 25 and 43, the teacher called a volunteer to make a model for the number 16. Ingrid volunteered but did not know what to do when she got up.

(32) T: Can someone help her?
(33) Kevin: 1 ten. [Ingrid put down 1 ten.]
(34) T: Right. We need to show 16.
(35) Kevin: 6 more.
(36) T: What are they called?
(37) Ss: Ones. [Ingrid put down 6 ones.]

The three modeling activities (i.e., modeling 25, 43, and 16) to this point seemed to be consistent with the teacher's stated goal that students would learn to "represent a number with a model." The purpose of such activities though was unclear. In other words, we do not know what mathematical idea(s) students were to learn from participating in such activities. After Ingrid finished modeling the number 16 with the help of her classmates, the teacher returned to the number 25.

(38) T: We are going to make a model drawing a picture for the number 25.
[She draws]

$$= \frac{\text{Tens}}{2} \quad \frac{\text{Ones}}{5}$$

(39) T: This is my place value chart, ones have a special place, tens have a special place. That means if I put five here [pointing to the ones place], it has a special value. What is it?
(40) Ss: 5.
(41) T: How many tens do I have?
(42) Ss: 10, 20, 2.
(43) T: 2. How many fives?[2]
(44) Ss: 5.

At this point, the teacher appeared ready to teach the concept of place value, but the teacher simply mentioned, "This is my place value chart, ones have a special place, tens have a special place." In this example (i.e., 25), the teacher never pointed out that 25 is a two-digit number that consists of 2 at its tens place and 5 at its ones place. And the place (or position) of 2 or 5 determines their values. For instance, 2 is at the tens place, therefore, it represents 2 tens or 20 ones, but 5 is at the ones place, therefore it represents 5 ones. Because of this, we can decompose 25 as 2 tens and 5 ones. This would naturally lead to the teacher's introduction of "Say a number in three different ways." Instead, after the teacher made the statement about the place value chart, the teacher continued with modeling more two-digit numbers. Then the teacher told the students to take out their math books, missing the opportunity to discuss the utility of place value.

(45) T: Let's look at the first model. Put your finger on it. How many tens do you see?
(46) G: 3.
(47) T: 3 tens. How many ones?
(48) Kevin: 4.
(49) T: We have 3 tens and 4 ones. What number does that make?
(50) G: 34.
(51) T: This first one looks a little different. 3 tens 4 ones = 34. Another way of saying 34 is 30 + 4. And we can write 34. We can say it in three different ways.

The teacher then led the class through the problems in the math book in the same manner. Although the students could write a number, say, 94, in three different ways as: (1) 9 tens 4 ones = 94, or (2) 90 + 4 = 94, or (3) 94, they probably did not understand the purpose of such exercises, because they were not explicitly taught the underlying mathematical concept, namely, the concept of place value and the relationships among different digits within the same number (in this case, two-digit numbers).

The observations so far indicated that the mathematical ideas introduced to the students in these two lessons were mostly taught in a fragmented way. Naturally some students may not even understand the procedural part of the concepts they had learned, as shown in the beginning of the third lesson (see below). In this third lesson, the teacher was reviewing with the students what they had learned in the previous two lessons. The teacher gave several two-digit numbers and asked the students the numbers of tens and ones in each number. When the teacher gave the number 19 and asked how many tens, a few students yelled out "9", "19", and "10 ones"; when the teacher asked how many ones, one student gave "2" while another student said, "I forgot." The review was a nice check for student understanding: however, little opportunities were provided to correct student misunderstanding.

The focus of the third lesson, as the teacher stated, was for students to "understand the difference between a digit and a number. The value of a number depends on the place value of the digit." The second part of the teacher's response makes us wonder whether the teacher has a clear understanding of the difference between a digit and a number. The statement that "the value of a number depends on the place value of the digit" is mathematically confusing, because comparing the values of different numbers has nothing to do with the place value. It is when we compare the values of different digits within a multi-digit number that the place value of each of the digits matters.

Furthermore, the way the teacher helped students to "understand the difference between a digit and a number" was stated as a matter of fact, as the following interactional episode shows:

(52) T: Let's say I want this number. Raise your hand and tell me this number. [T wrote on board.] 63.

(53) B: 63.

(54) T: And this number? [T wrote] 36.

(55) Desiree: 3.

(56) T: Place value chart

	Tens	Ones
I have a 6 and a 3 here.	6	3
I have a 3 and 6 here.	3	6

I have two digits in both. Is it the same number?

(57) Ss: No.

(58) Ss: Yes.

(59) T: It is? Okay. I owe you $63 but I'm only going to pay you $36.

(60) B: No, that's a lot of money.

(61) T: Each numeral is called a digit. We write digits [writes] 0, 1, 2, 3, 4, 5, 6, 7, 8, 9. All digits can make all kinds of numbers. We call it a two-digit number. It has a 6 and a 3. We call this a two-digit number. It has a 3 and a 6. We call the whole thing a number. With a raised hand, show me on your fingers, how many digits in 36?

(62) Ss: 9, 4, 3.
[T repeated the digit and number explanation.]

(63) T: [wrote 126] How many digits?

(64) T/Ss: [count together] 1, 2, 3.

(65) T: It makes a difference where we put our digits on our place value chart.

As shown in the above episode, the concepts of digit and number were not explained clearly to the students. The teacher simply stated "I have two digits in both [63 and 36]." No wonder when the teacher asked "Is it the same number?" (i.e., "Are 63 and 36 the same number?"), some students were confused and said "yes." It is possible that they thought the teacher meant, "Do 63 and 36 both have two digits?" since the teacher had just said "I have two digits in both." The teacher used a money example (i.e., the difference between $63 and $36) to help students understand that the two numbers were not the same. However, instead of explaining why they are different, the teacher made a statement that digits 0–9 can make all kinds of numbers without really helping students to understand what this means. The rest of the lesson continued with the teacher modeling two-digit numbers and asking students "How many tens? How many ones?"

The classroom interactional episodes from this 2nd grade class showed that the fundamental concept of how numbers are composed in the decimal numeral system was treated in a fragmented and disconnected way. The students may have learned that 1 ten equals 10 ones, or that 10 ones make 1 ten, or that 36 can be represented as 30 + 6 or 3 tens and 6 ones, but were not led to discover or understand the utility of place value. Students left the series of lessons without understanding the concept of place value within the decimal system. This is critical since the place value concept not only enables them to see how numbers are composed (i.e., the relationship between different digits of the same number), but also prepares them for a soon-to-be-learned topic, namely regrouping.

Second Grade Class: Two-Digit Subtraction with Regrouping—Do Students Understand the Application of the Place Value Concept in This Context?

Three weeks after the observation of the first 2nd grade class, a second 2nd grade class was observed for three consecutive days. At the time of our observations, this 2nd grade class was learning two-digit subtraction with regrouping. The first of the three lessons introduced the steps of regrouping, whereas the second lesson focused on subtraction of two-digit numbers with 0 in the ones place. The third lesson reviewed the first two lessons. The focus of the first lesson, as the teacher stated, was to "subtract two-digit numbers, regrouping when necessary, deciding if they need to regroup, remember the steps of regrouping."

After reviewing with the students that "difference in mathematics" means "the correct answer to a subtraction problem," the teacher writes the word "regroup" on the board.

(66) Ss: Regroup.
(67) T: What do we call it when we're adding?
(68) G: Carry.
(69) T: [writes Carry] What about take away?
(70) Ss: Borrowing.
(71) T: [writes Borrowing].

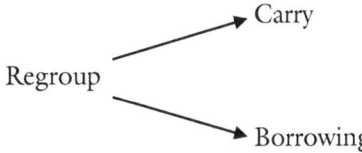

(72) T: Guys, guess what? Regroup can mean either one.
    [T gets cubes/blocks, puts 10 single cubes on the table].
(73) T: My friends, how many do I have here? I'll help you count [picking up the cubes so Ss can see better].
(74) T/Ss: 1, 2, 3, 4, 5, 6, 7, 8, 9, 10.
(75) T: How many do I have here? [Holds a 10 block].
(76) Ss: 10.
(77) T: So which has more?
(78) Ss: Same.
(79) T: So I can take this [holds the 10 block], saw it and get 10 little cubes, or I can take these 10 [holds 10 single cubes], glue them together and get this [holds the 10 block].
(80) T: Carry means putting together and borrowing is taking apart. I don't know if Ms. M [the sub] explained that very well, because regrouping can mean either one.

In this interaction, the concept of regrouping as applied in addition and subtraction problems was merely taught as a fact, namely, regrouping is called "carrying" when we are adding and "borrowing" when we take away (i.e., in subtraction). Furthermore, the relationship between the two different applications of the same concept was not explained but merely stated as "Guys, guess what? Regroup can mean either one." In fact, helping students to understand the concept and application of regrouping is closely related to the fundamental idea of how numbers are composed in the decimal system. Helping students to understand the connection between two different applications of the same mathematical concept (i.e., regrouping) in addition (i.e., carrying—composing) and subtraction (i.e., borrowing—decomposing) would enable them to learn something of lasting value, rather than a mere fact that regrouping is called carrying in addition but borrowing in subtraction.

Although the teacher tried to use the manipulative to convey the idea that regrouping "can mean either one," the approach did not facilitate students' understanding because the connection between the manipulative activities and the mathematical concepts was never made explicit. In other words, the way the manipulative was used showed no connection between the visual symbols (i.e., breaking a 10 block into 10 pieces or gluing 10 pieces of cubes together) and the mathematical idea of carrying in addition (composing) or borrowing in subtraction (decomposing). Therefore, without a conceptual understanding of how regrouping works in different situations, students have learned the concept in a procedural way. A lack of students' conceptual understanding was apparent when the teacher tried to progress, only to discover that the students were not ready to move on. The teacher assessed students' understanding, but only at the level of recitation. Indeed, some students had memorized the script, though few had learned what the script meant, as shown in the following episode.

(81) T: We worked on some problems like this [wrote]

Tens	Ones
4	5
−2	7

(82) T: If you don't remember then you need to pay really good attention.

(83) T: If it helps you, you can draw a line. [Drew dotted line down between tens and ones column in the above problem.]

(84) T: What is the first thing we do in a subtraction problem? [Half the class raises hands.] It starts with the word "look." Taylor.

(85) Taylor: Look at the ones.

(86) T: Look at the ones. You can't even think about take away until you think about the ones. Always start on the right. Reading we go from left to right, but this is backwards from reading. We go right to left. Step 1, what is it?

(87) Ss: Look at the ones.

(88) T: We are looking at subtraction. Step 1, say it.

(89) Ss: Look at the ones.

(90) T: [wrote and said] Look at the ones.

(91) T: Marvin, why are we looking at the ones? What are we looking for?

(92) Marvin: [quiet].

(93) T: Marvin, would you like to pick someone who has their hand up? [Half had hands up.]

(94) Marvin: Samantha.

(95) Samantha: To see if you need to regroup.

(96) T: [wrote, adds to step 1, Look at the ones: to see if you need to regroup].
Now what's step 1? Say it.

(97) Ss: Look at the ones to see if you need to regroup.

(98) T: What's step 1? Vanessa.

(99) Vanessa: Look at the ones to see if you need to regroup.

(100) T: What's step 1? [Pointing to another girl.]

(101) G: Look at the ones to see if you need to regroup.

(102) T: What's step 1? Jonathan.

(103) Jonathan: Look at the ones to see if you need to regroup.

(104) T: How do I know? [Half raised hands.] Keano?

(105) Keano: [mumbles].

(106) T: Can someone tell me in a different way? Taylor?

(107) Taylor: Top number, take away bottom number.

(108) T: Top number, take away bottom number. Say it!

(109) Ss: Top number, take away bottom number.

(110) T: That's why we look at the ones.

In the above interaction, the teacher relied heavily on rote learning (i.e., memorization of steps) to teach students the steps of conducting subtraction. Once the students firmly memorized step 1, the class moved on.

(111) T: Everybody, let's talk to Mr. 4.

(112) Ss: Mr. 4.

(113) T: Ask him if you can have one of his tens.

(114) Ss: Mr. 4, can I have one of your tens?

(115) T: Yes, you may, but how many will you leave me? Paul?

(116) Paul: 3.

(117) T: [wrote 3 in the box above 4]. Am I done? Marvin?

(118) Marvin: No.

(119) T: What do I put up here? [Pointed to the box above 5.]

(120) Ss: 15.

(121) T: [wrote 15]. Why did I put 15 in this box? Fernando?

(122) Fernando: [quiet].

(123) T: I used to have [drew 5 circles]. Then I borrowed [drew 10 more circles]. Now I have 15. You can do it quicker by putting a 1 in front of the 5 [demonstrated].

(124) T: We have to do all these steps just to get ready to subtract. Now we're ready to subtract.

(125) T: Now, what am I going to subtract? Fernando, what do I subtract?

(126) Fernando: 7.

(127) T: What am I going to take 7 away from? Don't tell me the answer, I will be very upset. Daniel, am I taking away from 5?

(128) Daniel: No.

(129) T: Daniel, what am I taking away from?

(130) Daniel: [quiet].

(131) T: Taylor, what am I taking away from?

(132) Taylor: 15.

(133) T: What's 15 take away 7?

(134) Ss: 8.

(135) T: [puts down 8] Am I done?

(136) Ss: No.

(137) T: Marvin, what do I do? [Class quiet.] Everybody say it out loud.

(138) Ss: 3 take away 2 is 1.

(139) T: [puts down 1 in the tens place].

The regrouping (i.e., borrowing, decomposing) step, as shown in this episode, was not taught for understanding at all, because the two digits (4 and 5) in the number 45 were treated as if they were independent neighbors. If we do not have enough ones in 5 to take away 7, we can simply go to our neighbor, Mr. 4, to borrow one of his tens. If so, what are we going to return later to Mr. 4? We have emphasized that mathematically 4 and 5 in 45 are two inter-related components of one number due to the way numbers are composed in the decimal system. In addition, when we have too many ones in the ones place, we compose them into units of 10 and put them in the tens place. Consequently, when we do not have enough ones to carry out the subtraction, we can decompose the tens back into ones. On the surface, this procedure seems similar to what was used in this class, yet the underlying concept is completely different. Composing/decomposing explains the concept of place value underlying the algorithm, whereas borrowing a ten from Mr. 4 does not. In language that 2nd graders could understand, Mr. 40 needs to change his name to Mr. 30 plus 10. This representation at least captures correctly the concept of decomposition. The sole procedural approach to conducting two-digit subtractions with regrouping failed to help this group of students to understand the basic concept and may have reinforced their misunderstanding. After practicing the same procedure with different two-digit subtractions, the teacher asked, "Do we always have to regroup?" The students replied, "Yes." These students were so well trained on the procedures taught that they thought they needed to follow the same procedures in all kinds of two-digit subtractions.

Since the concept underlying the algorithm (i.e., place value and regrouping) was never made explicit to the students, two-digit subtractions with zero in the ones place was treated as a separate topic, even though conceptually nothing new is involved in such applications. The focus of the second lesson, as the teacher stated, was "subtracting with zero in the ones place, deciding if they need to regroup, and remember the steps of regrouping." The steps that were taught in the previous lesson were used.

(140) T: [wrote]

$$\begin{array}{r} 70 \\ -24 \\ \hline \end{array}$$

(141) T: Nothing changes. What's step 1?
(142) Ss: Look at the ones to see if you need to regroup.

(143) T: Since ...

(144) Ss: The bigger number is on the bottom...

(145) T: Is the bigger one on the bottom?

(146) Ss: Yes.

(147) T: Do you need to regroup?

(148) Ss: Yes.

(149) T: Now here's the tricky part, but it's not that tricky. If you have no cookies can you take 4 away?

(150) Ss: No.

(151) T: Let's talk.

(152) Ss: Mr. 7 can I borrow one of your tens?

(153) T: Yes, you can, but how many will you leave me?

(154) Ss: 6.

(155) T: [crossed out 7, replaced with 6].

(156) B1: Put 10 in the box.

(157) T: [turned 0 into 10].

(158) T: The only time you can put 10 is if there is a 0. Let's go, talk with me.

(159) Ss: 10 take away 4 is 6, 6 take away 2 is 4.

(160) T: Ariana, I think you will learn more if you pay attention. Say it.

(161) Ariana: 10 take away 4 is 6, 6 take away 2 is 4.

(162) T: [wrote 46].

(163) T: That's not so hard. Now I have a question. Is there a time when there is a zero and I don't have to regroup? Daniel, what do you think? Is there a time when there is a zero and I don't have to regroup? When would that be? Can you give me an example?

(164) Daniel: 10.

(165) T: [wrote]

$$\begin{array}{r} 70 \\ -10 \\ \hline \end{array}$$

(166) T: Paul, what do you think? Right or wrong?

(167) Paul: Wrong.

(168) T: Let's pretend I looked at that and said, "Do I need to regroup?"

(169) Ss: Mr. 7, can I borrow one of your tens?
(170) T: Yes, you can, but how many will you leave me?
(171) Ss: 6.
(172) T: [crossed out 7, replaced with 6. Crossed out 0, replaced with 10].

$$6\ 10$$

$$\not{7}\ |\ \not{0}$$

$$\underline{-1\ |0}$$

$$10$$

(173) T: When you see a number like that [pointed to the bottom 10], there's a problem because the biggest number you can have is a 9. The rule didn't change. Is the bottom number bigger?
(174) G: Same.
(175) T: Can I have zero and take away none of them?
(176) Ss: Yes.

As shown in this episode, the teacher decomposed 1 ten in the number 70 into 10 ones and said, "The only time you can put 10 is if there is a 0," which is not true. Although the standard procedure in most two-digit subtractions with regrouping would normally combine the decomposed 10 ones with other ones (e.g., in 53 − 17 we would normally decompose 53 into 40 + 13), we do not have to. In fact, we could regroup 53 as 40 + 10 + 3 and conduct the subtraction in this way. In the tens place, 40 minus 10 equals 30, whereas in the ones place, 10 minus 7 is 3, plus 3 that is originally in the ones place, we would get 6. So the final answer would be 36. Of course, the second approach of regrouping 53 (i.e., 40 + 10 + 3) is unconventional, but perfectly correct. In fact, unconventional approaches such as this are widely used in daily mental arithmetic calculations. It is unfortunate for the teacher to lead students to believe what is typically done is the only correct way to solve the problem. Another example is that the teacher told the students that the big number is always on top (as in 72 − 54). When she asked what if she switched 72 with 54, the students yelled out "Math jail!" Even though at 2nd grade students are not taught how to subtract a bigger number from a smaller one, they should not be confused by the false idea that the big number is always on top and therefore 54 minus 72 is wrong.

The second point worth mentioning is that when the teacher asked the class "Is there a time when there is a zero and I don't have to regroup?" Daniel gave an example of 10 (in 70 − 10). The teacher asked Paul why the example was right and Paul replied, "Wrong." Without inviting Paul to explain why he thought the example as wrong (i.e., Paul thinks that one needs to regroup in 70 − 10), the teacher led the class through the same procedures. Now the class found out that they would get 10 ones in the ones place when they regrouped 70 as 60 plus 10. At this point, the teacher simply stated, "When you see a number like that, there's a problem because the biggest number you can have is a 9. The rule didn't change." There was no attempt to help students understand why we do not leave 10 units in the ones place, which would have led directly to the fundamental idea of how numbers are composed in the decimal system. Perhaps Paul was thinking to decompose 70 as 60 plus 10, therefore, "70 − 10" becomes "60 + 10 − 10" which gives 60. This would be an alternative approach to solving the problem that is perfectly correct.

As we have seen so far the concept of regrouping was never taught for conceptual understanding, but as a set of fixed computational steps. The third math lesson just reinforced students in these steps. In the end, students may or may not memorize these steps, or they may just automatically apply these steps regardless of whether it is necessary or not. For instance, some students automatically applied the regrouping procedures in 36 − 24 even though no regrouping is needed to do the subtraction.

The two 2nd grade classes described up to this point give us a picture of how little opportunities the students were given to learn the mathematical ideas of tens and ones, and regrouping in two-digit subtractions. This happened because the teaching was fragmented and procedural driven and did not emphasize mathematical reasoning or conceptual understanding. The teacher never explained or led students to discover the fundamental mathematical ideas underlying the lessons: (1) how numbers are composed in the decimal system; (2) regrouping in addition and subtraction; (3) the relationship between how numbers are composed in the decimal system and its implication for regrouping in addition or subtraction; and (4) the relationship between the application of the same concept (regrouping) in two reverse mathematical operations (addition and subtraction). Naturally, students taught in this way will most likely be unable to extend their learned knowledge to new situations (i.e., knowledge transfer).

Teaching students a key to solving problems will enable students to go a long way (Ma 1999, 2010). When we confine students with all kinds of mathematical statements, rules, or facts, they will not be equipped to succeed on their own when confronted with more complicated mathematical problems. As shown in one of the instructional episodes, two-digit subtractions with 0 on the ones place was treated as a separate topic. Unfortunately, we saw evidence that these misunderstandings are repeated, not replaced, as students get older. The same procedures we observed in those two 2nd grade classes were used by 4th grade teachers teaching four-digit subtractions.

Fourth Grade Class: Four-Digit Addition and Subtractions with Regrouping—Do Students See the Same Application of the Place Value Concept with "Bigger" Numbers?

At the time of our observations, this 4th grade class was learning four-digit addition and subtraction that involved regrouping. The first of the three lessons introduced the steps of carrying out four-digit addition and subtraction. The second lesson reviewed the topics of the first lesson and the last lesson was about subtracting numbers with zeros.

The following episode was from the first lesson and showed how four-digit addition and subtraction was introduced to the students.

On board: Add and subtract four-digit numbers using regrouping.

9910	9910	6899	9674	8902	9201
+7340	−7340	+2267	−1406	−5730	+1321

(177) T: Can I start anywhere?
(178) Christian: You have to start in the ones column.
(179) T: [wrote 0, 5] Can I squeeze 12 in there?

$$\begin{array}{r} 9910 \\ +7340 \\ \hline {}_{12}50 \end{array}$$

(180) Ss: No.
(181) T: Why?
(182) Ss: You have to regroup.

(183) T: [uses manipulatives] I have 12 hundreds. I can't put it all in the hundreds place, so I put 1 in the thousands place, and have 2 left over so I put the 2 down.

$$9910$$
$$+7340$$
$$17250$$

(184) T: Can we have less talking? It takes too much time. Now we are regrouping in the thousands. Now we'll do it with subtraction.

$$9910$$
$$-7340$$

(185) T: Where do I start?
(186) Ss: Ones.
(187) T: Tamara, can we take away 4 from 1 in the tens column? No. We regroup in the next column and change the 9 to 8 and this becomes 11. 11 take away 4?
(188) Ss: 8.
(189) Chase: 7.
(190) T: Good. Check before you call out. [Class moved on.]
(191) Erica: 5.
(192) Jeremy: 2.
(193) T: Did we get closer? Yes, because this number rounded would be 3000.

The addition problem the class worked on (i.e., 9910 + 7340) involves two places where one would need to regroup. The first regrouping was composing 10 hundreds in the hundreds place into 1 thousand and put it in the thousands place. The teacher asked the class, "Can I squeeze 12 in there?" and "Why?" The students knew the answer (i.e., they cannot squeeze 12 in the hundreds place), but could not explain why, because they were never taught why. The teacher did not help to enhance students' understanding. As can be seen in her comments (line 183), she described the procedure of regrouping, but not the reason why we need to regroup. As explained when discussing the 2nd grade cases, the reason why we regroup has to do with how numbers are formed in the decimal system. This fundamental idea was never made explicit to the students in any of the three classes where the focus of the lessons was on regrouping.

Another point worth mentioning is that although the teacher demonstrated the procedures of four-digit subtraction and addition using the same numbers, the connection between how regrouping was used in these two inverse mathematical operations (i.e., addition and subtraction) was never discussed. The students were never given the opportunity to learn that regrouping in addition involves composing 10 units of lower place value into 1 unit of the immediate next higher place value, whereas regrouping in subtraction involves decomposing 1 unit of higher place value into 10 units of the immediate next lower place value. It was not clear whether the teacher understood the relationship, because at the beginning of the lesson, the teacher said, "We will also be practicing addition and subtraction of four-digit numbers using regrouping. Regrouping is to borrow from the next place value. Does anyone remember what sum means?" The definition of regrouping that the teacher described here applies only to subtractions, but the teacher immediately asked the students if they remembered what sum means. This was confusing and left us wondering whether the teacher thinks regrouping means the same thing in both applications (i.e., in addition and subtraction).

Because the students were never taught to understand conceptually how regrouping works in either mathematical operation (i.e., addition and subtraction), these students could only be expected to recall memorized procedures and carry out the operations. Some students, however, would have difficulties, particularly in conducting subtractions with regrouping. As our observations showed, at the end of the first lesson, quite a few students did not know how to subtract four-digit numbers that involve regrouping. What they did was simply switching the digits to make an easier problem that did not involve regrouping. For instance, one student did not know how to compute $3204 - 2413$, so what this student did was simply change the problem into $3414 - 2203$ (i.e., switch 1 and 4 in 2413 with 0 and 2 in 3204 respectively).

Original :   What the student did :

3204	3414
−2413	−2203
791	1211

The teacher noticed this common practice among some students and decided to use a "real-life" example to show why they should not do that.

(194) T: Everyone, get to your seats and wait for corrections. Tonight's homework will be more practice of four-digit adding and subtracting. A common error is inverting the numbers. Maybe you think regrouping takes too much work. Don't flip the problem around. It's going to be wrong. If I go to a department store and the cashier says, "That's 54.35." I give her a $100 bill and cashier gives me a $5 dollar bill. The cashier says, "I don't feel like regrouping."

$$100.00$$
$$-54.35$$
$$4.35$$

(195) Ss: That's a rip off.
(196) T: Right. You have to learn this so you don't get ripped off.

First of all, the teacher did not conduct the calculation correctly, if she were to demonstrate the same switching practice that some students were doing. Using these students' practice, $100 subtract $54.35 would give us $154.35 instead of $4.35. So the cashier would give back more change than necessary (the correct change should be $45.65). Of course, if the teacher followed the exact procedure that these students used, she would not be able to convey the message that they were being ripped off. Second, instead of helping the students understand the correct procedure, the teacher simply concluded that they had to learn this so they would not get ripped off.

During the second lesson, the teacher reviewed four-digit addition and subtraction with the students, going over the rules of regrouping:

(197) T: We're going to regroup 10 ones into one 10. We'll put the zero down here and the 1 in the box. This doesn't mean you're not smart, it just means you need practice.
(198) T: Step 2: [T read] Put the 2 down and carry the 1 into the hundreds place. [T continued Step 3 and Step 4.]

If the same approach of how regrouping was taught to the students did not work in the first lesson, it certainly would not work when it was used again, because the approach focused on the procedure, not on the understanding. The teacher, however, seemed to believe that understanding would arise simply from more practice, because the activities of the second lesson were merely applying the four-steps in different three- or four-digit addition and subtraction problems. An opportunity was lost to explore and understand the reasons for students' mistakes, an understanding which could help to correct the misunderstanding.

Earlier we have showed that two-digit subtraction with zero in the ones place was treated as a special topic and was the focus of one whole lesson in the 2nd grade class. Similarly, subtraction involving multi-digit numbers with zeros was treated as a separate topic and took one whole lesson to learn in this 4th grade class.

The focus of the third lesson, as the teacher stated, was "subtracting numbers with zeros (regrouping zeros)."

On board—Subtracting numbers with zeros using regrouping.

300	900	600	100	300	1000	3000	7100	1000	5000	3000
−12	−374	−211	−29	−287	−384	−2241	−3291	−328	−3024	−280

51000	6000	5000	8000
−3906	−2900	−2630	7887

(199) T: Over the past few days we've been practicing regrouping in addition and subtraction. I noticed a part that's a little more difficult for everyone. When I was in 4th grade, anytime we had a problem with zeros my teacher said cross it out and put in a 9. I had no idea why I did it. When I became a teacher I learned in the teaching manual, why. I never understood it. I don't want you to be like me. I'm going to attempt to show you two different ways. The first problem is:

$$\begin{array}{r} 300 \\ -12 \\ \hline \end{array}$$

(200) T: Subtract what's on the bottom from the top row. Can we take it from the tens column? No. Can we borrow from the hundreds column? Yes. How much is it worth?

(201) Ss: 10.

(202) Ss: 4.

(203) T: It's always 10, change the 1 to 10 ones. I traded 1 ten for 10 ones.

$$\begin{array}{r} 2\ 91 \\ \cancel{3}\,\cancel{0}\,0 \\ -1\ 2 \\ \hline 2\ 8\ 8 \end{array}$$

(204) T: Here's where the 9 comes from.

Although the teacher told the students that she was going to show them two different ways, she actually only demonstrated one way as described in this interaction. She repeated the same approach using a different example (900 − 374), if that was what she meant. The teacher intended to help the students understand how regrouping was typically conducted when both the ones and the tens places are zero in three-digit subtraction, because she never understood this as a student as she courageously shared with her students. The way the teacher explained the concepts to the students, however, might not be helpful for their understanding. First, why 10 when one goes from one place value to the next immediate left place value was not made clear to the students. The teacher simply stated, "It's always 10." Second, how was 300 decomposed as 2 in the hundreds place, 9 and 1 in the tens place was not explained to the students. The teacher simply told the student "change the 1 to 10 ones. I traded 1 ten for 10 ones." Given that students in this class were still struggling with regrouping, the teacher could have pointed out that once she decomposed 1 unit in the hundreds place into 10 units in the tens place, she then regrouped 10 ten as 9 tens and 1 ten. This 1 ten was further decomposed into 10 units into the ones place so that we can subtract 2 from 10 in the ones place, and 1 from 9 in the tens place. The teacher never explained clearly where 9 and 1 came from and why.

It is quite possible that this teacher did not really understand the fundamental idea of how numbers are composed in the decimal system, as she told her students so at the beginning of the lesson. For the reminder of the lesson the teacher kept reminding students, "I'll check my neighbor and if I get some I'll lend it to you. What do you always give? Magic number?" So 10 became a magic number instead of being explained as the rate of change from one place value to the immediate next place value in the decimal system. Furthermore, whenever 1 unit was "borrowed" (using the teacher's term), it was automatically rewritten as 9 and 1 without explaining clearly to the students why. No wonder when a student was called to solve 1000 − 384, the student automatically wrote:

$$1\ 1\ 1$$
$$\not{1}\,0\ 0\ 0$$

It was obvious that the student did not understand how regrouping works in this context. In fact, a lot of students in this class probably did not understand either, since the teacher commented "I still see a lot of errors. We're still not ready to go on our own yet." The teacher led the class to practice more exercises of the same nature. But students may never be able to strike out on their own if they are not equipped with the key to problem solving. These critical instructional episodes from three different elementary classrooms showed how a basic mathematical idea was taught. The observations repeatedly showed that mathematics is being treated as set of isolated facts, rules, and steps. In these classrooms, it seems that learning mathematics simply means mastering these disconnected facts, rules, and steps. Acquiring these facts, rules, and steps with accuracy and fluency equals understanding. Therefore, mathematics understanding is regarded as arising automatically from repeated practice.

Students taught in this way will rarely achieve the deep understanding called for by the Common Core State Standards for mathematics, or others like them. Making meaning requires a systematic presentation of concepts that makes transparent their many interconnections. When students move on from grade to grade with poor foundational skills, mathematics mastery becomes increasingly difficult. The foundation is insufficient to build understanding. Moreover, it is difficult for students experiencing this type of mathematics teaching to develop confidence in themselves as problem solvers and thinkers. Students lack mathematical reasoning skills because they are not taught these skills. Classroom conversations about mathematics where students take an active role are rare, which is also evident and permeates the secondary math classes, including the Honors classes. The next two cases came from an 8th grade Algebra 1 class and a high school Honors Algebra 2 class.

Beyond x's and y's: Dynamics of the Middle and High School Algebra Classes

The first series of instructional episodes was taken from an 8th grade Algebra 1 class. Students in this class were on the two-year Algebra 1 pathway, which means that these students were not as advanced as those who complete the same course within one year. The Honors Algebra 2 class, on the contrary, consisted of mostly advanced students. Despite perhaps big differences in student population in terms of academic ability, the underlying classroom discourse was similar in many aspects.

An 8th Grade Class: Algebra 1—Do Students See the Different Forms of Representations (Numbers and Number Line; Symbols and Definitions)?

As the class started, the teacher gave the students a warm-up activity:

Warm up

1. $12 + 3x$ when $x = 0$
2. $12 + 3x$ when $x = 1$
3. $12 + 3x$ when $x = 2$
4. $12 + 3x$ when $x = 3$

[Ss opened their notebooks and began working on the warm up.]

(205) T: I am going to do number 3 for you as an example. [Wrote on OHP] $12 + 3x$ when $x = 2$.

(206) T: [Wrote and said] $12 + 3$ times 2. This gives us [wrote $12 + 6 = 18$].

[Several Ss visited the pencil sharpener to sharpen their pencils. This disrupted the instruction.]

(207) T: Please pay attention!

[Ss continued working on the warm up.]
[Ss became extremely noisy.]

(208) T: Stop talking! You are 8th graders. [T had a confrontation with a boy for leaving his book at home.] The exercise you are doing is worth 10 points. Okay, three more minutes.

(209) T: Look at number 1. It's 12 + 3 times 0. This gives us [wrote 12 + 0 = 12]. 12 + 3 times 1. [T went through all the warm-up exercises in the same manner].

(210) T: Open your books to page 59. This is an open book test. [T put a slide on the OHP.]

Test problems:
Evaluate the variable expression when y = 3 and x = 5.

1. $5y + x^2$ 3. $2y + 9x - 7$
2. $24 / (y - x)$ 4. $(5y + x) / 4$

In exercises 5–7, write the expression in exponential form.

5. 5y.5y.5y.5y.
6. Nine cubed.
7. Six to the nth power.
8. Insert grouping symbols in 5. 4 + 6 so that the value of the expression is 50.

Express as a variable, an equation or an inequality expression.

8. 7 times an n.
9. 9 is less than t.
10. 8 minus s is 4.
11. y decreases by 3.

(211) T: You have 15 minutes on this test.

As shown in this instructional episode, to help students work through the warm-up exercise, the teacher first demonstrated the calculation steps using 12 + 3x when x = 2 as an example. The students were then on their own. Once time was up, the teacher gave out the calculations and answers to each problem. There was no interaction between the teacher and the students about mathematics. All interactions pertained to disciplinary problems. Furthermore, when the warm-up activity was over, the students were given an open book test that consisted of dry and meaningless drill exercises. After the test, the teacher spent the rest of the class time reviewing with the students "how to arrange numbers according to the ascending and descending order of a number."

(212) T: You must copy your new words.

New words

- Real number
- Real number line
- Positive number 5
- Negative number 5
- Integer + or − number 5
- Whole number
- Graph of a number

(213) T: [Wrote on board] 3, 4, 5, 1. I draw a number line and locate these numbers on it.

0 _ 1 _ 2 _ 3 _ 4 _ 5 . This is all you are supposed to do. I gave you a series of numbers to arrange in ascending order. Now I am going to give you numbers to arrange in descending order [wrote on board] −4, 5, −3, 6, −1, 2, −2. Put these on a number line.

[Observer note: After a minute or so, I walked around. One girl counted her money rather than working on the assignment. Another boy, balled paper and used the trashcan for a basketball basket. Three boys in the back row played instead of working on the assignment. I estimated that about 10% students tried to do the assignment].

(214) T: [Wrote on board]

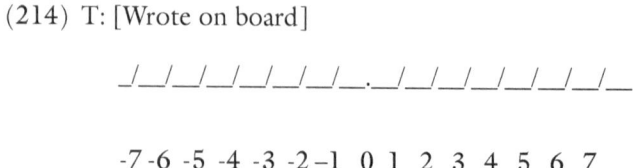

-7 -6 -5 -4 -3 -2 –1 0 1 2 3 4 5 6 7

(215) T: [pointed to the right of 0] If you move this way you increase and decrease if you move this way [pointed to the left of 0]. What are the numbers on the left?
(216) G: Negative.
(217) T: Right. The only time that's not negative or positive is 0.

Again in this example, we see that the teacher first demonstrated how to arrange numbers on a number line using an example that consisted of 3, 4, 5, 1. The students then are simply told, "This is all you are supposed to do" and were on their own. After giving students some time to work on their own (as we can see from the description, the majority of the students were off task), the teacher showed them the answer. There was one interaction where the teacher asked, "What are the numbers on the left?" When a student gave the correct answer (i.e., negative), the teacher said, "Right."

In terms of discourse of teaching and learning mathematics, mathematics instruction in this Algebra class is remarkably similar to that in elementary classes. Mathematical concepts and ideas (in this case, x's and y's or numbers) were given to the students through drills. There was no connection among different activities. The teacher was the center of instruction in each activity, demonstrating how to solve a problem and assigning problems of the same kind for the students to practice. The students' role in learning was to execute correctly the same procedures or steps that the teacher had shown. In this 8th grade class, there were almost no conversations about mathematics.

As mentioned earlier, students in this class were not advanced. Indeed, our observations showed that these 8th graders possessed very poor foundational mathematical (or arithmetic) skills. For instance, when the teacher called on several students to give the answer to $15 - 12/3 + 17$, only one student was able to give the correct answer. Poor foundational skills of students in combination with their lack of interest in classwork (there were constant disruptive behaviors in this class) make the task of teaching Algebra for understanding even more daunting. Now let us go into a high school Honors Algebra 2 class to see what mathematics teaching and learning looks like. Since it was an Honors Algebra 2 class, one would expect to see a quite different picture from the one we saw in the 8th grade Algebra 1 class.

A High School Class: Honors Algebra 2—Do Students See Different Forms of Representations (Equation and Its Graph) and Are They Able to Solve a Problem that Involves the Place Value Concept?

The teacher began by stating the purpose of the lesson as, "graphing linear equations using only the x and y intercepts, and graphing absolute value functions." After telling several students that they were going to demonstrate the next day how to solve one problem in the previous day's homework, the teacher reviewed the signs of x's and y's (i.e., positive or negative) in the four quadrants of the Cartesian coordinate system. Then the teacher told the students to look at page 108 of the text:

(218) T: It says in Example 2, find and graph 5 solutions of 3x + 2y = 4. I am going to ask you to graph Ax + By = C. And I'm pretending that A, B, and C are positive. [T wrote]
Ax + By = C   A > 0 B > 0 C > 0
Let x = 0
By = C
Y = C/B. [Repeat for let y = 0.]
Y – intercept (0, C/B)   x – intercept (C/A)

(219) T: If I graph this I get more or less something like this. [Drew]

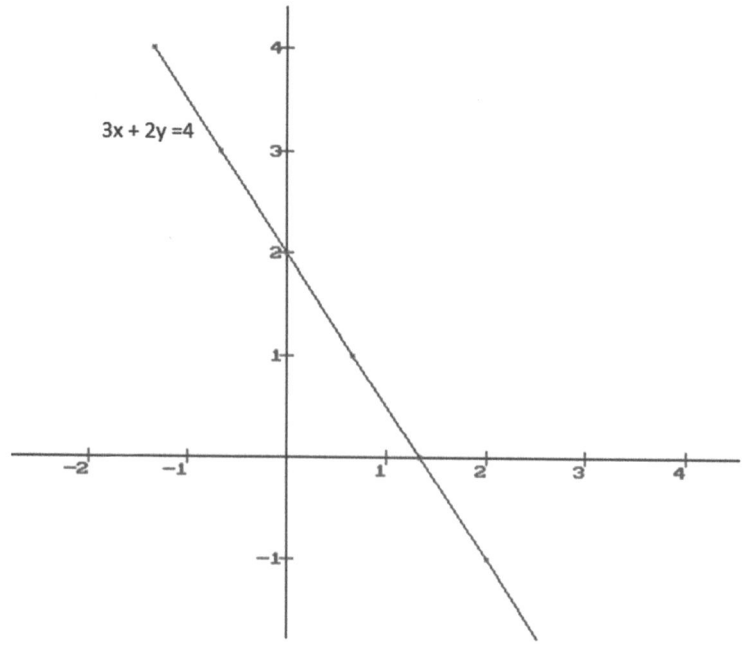

3x + 2y =4

(220) T: If I ask you to graph this one, 2x + 3y = 5. It looks like this, right? [Drew]

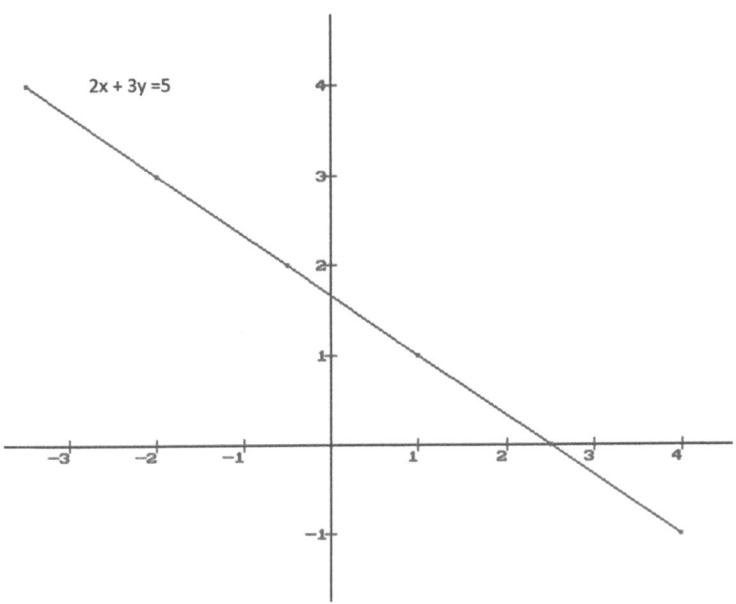

2x + 3y =5

(221) T: So you can graph anything with this system.

Once again, we see a similar approach of mathematics instruction, namely, the teacher demonstrating to students how to do something (in this context, how to graph a linear equation). Using the same approach, the teacher went over different examples in the text (e.g., how to graph y = x, y = |x|, y = −|x|, y = |x − a|, y = |x + a|, y =|x − a| + b, and y = −|x − a| + b). During these demonstrations, the teacher was the center of instruction, occasionally asking the students questions such as "What is the definition of absolute value?" or "If |y| = 5, then what would y equal?" After going through different examples in the text, the teacher finally came to the concept of "the slope of a line."

(222) T: Turn to page 112, 3.3, the slope of a line. What is a slope?
(223) G: The rise over run.
(224) T: The rise over run. When do you feel a slope?
        [No response from the students.]
(225) T: Is it when you go up a 100 storeys?

(226) Ss: Yes.
(227) T: If I take all of you outside and make you run up a hill, will you feel it?
(228) Ss: Yes.
(229) T: If I make you go up that hill 100 times, sprinting all the way, would you feel it?
(230) Ss: Yes.
(231) T: Yes, your heart would be pounding, right?
(232) Ss: Yes.
(233) T: So the slope, or the rise over run is what you would feel. If I picked two points, and called them P and Q, and P was at (1,1), and Q was at (2,2), they would look like this:

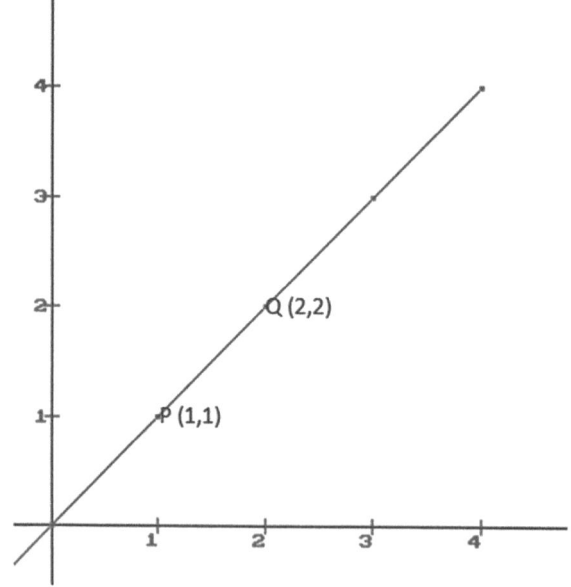

The subscripts just help differentiate the numbers.
The slope will be: slope = $(y_2 - y_1)/(x_2 - x_1)$.
(234) T: And I'm going to test you on the formula. So make sure you understand it. All of you know how to find the slope. So if I give you a slope like this:
Slope = $(1/2 - 3/2)/(5 - 2)$ (2,3 / 2) (5,1 / 2)
What would your slope be?

(235) Ss: $-1/3$.

The concept of "slope" is merely treated as "the rise over run," a correct formula definition yet one that hardly bears any meaning. The teacher tries to help the students "feel" a slope by giving examples such as "go up 100 storeys" and "run up a hill." These examples do not express the concept of slope. The formula for calculating the slope was given to the students who were told that they would be tested. It seems the expectation on the students was to memorize the formula and execute it with accuracy. But what does the formula mean? Why would the formula give the slope of a line? These questions were never discussed, because the concept of slope was narrowly defined as the rise over run instead of being conceptualized (in this context) as a rate that describes the linear relationship between variables x's and y's (i.e., amount of change in y for every unit change in x as the formula shows).

Obviously, the roles that the teacher and the students played in this lesson were essentially the same as the ones that we observed in the 8th grade Algebra 1 class. Students in this Honors Algebra 2 class, by definition, were far more advanced than those 8th graders who possessed very poor arithmetical skills. However, we have seen that even these advanced students typically were not experiencing the type of mathematics teaching and learning that reform asks for. Naturally, these students' opportunities to learn and to develop confidence in their own mathematical reasoning powers were limited, which can be seen shortly.

Earlier we mentioned that the teacher nominated several students who were going to demonstrate their solutions to a homework problem the next day. The following examples describe these students' demonstrations and explanations of their solutions. When these students were selected the day before the presentation, the teacher had indicated to them that, "You will be graded on the presentation and the correctness of your answer. To get the full 10 points for your answer, you will have to include all the steps it took to get that answer, and I will have to like the way you did it." The problem reads like this:

In Exercises 9–12, the digits of a positive two-digit integer N are interchanged to form an integer K. Find all possibilities for N under the conditions described:
Problem 9: N is odd and exceeds K by more than 18.

Kyle was the first one to present his solution, which is as follows:

Kyle's solution:

$N > K + 18$
$N = AB, K = BA$

$\underline{A}$

| $A < B$ | $A > 4$ | $\{4,5,6,7,8,9\}$ |
| $B = $ odd | $B = 1,3,5,7,9$ | $41, 51, 61, 71, 81, 91$ |

$\underline{B}$ $\{63,73,83,93,85,95\}$
$B < 5$
B odd $\{1, 3, 5\}$

(236) Kyle: It says that N is odd, the second digit is odd too. B is less than or equal to 5 or else it doesn't work. Because the number goes too high, so B has to be 1, 3, or 5.

(237) T: You lost me on that last bit. Can you go back and explain it?

(238) Kyle: The next number is 7 because it's going to be odd. Like 71 would be a number. If you flip it around, it would be 17. Then 71 + 18 would be more than the 17. So there's no number greater than 5 that would work. A is greater or equal to 4 or else it doesn't work in the problem. So 4, 5, 6, 7, 8, and 9. So 41 is going to be the first number. And 4 − 1 is 3 because this is A and this is B. A − B has to be greater than or equal to B in the problem, so 4 − 1 has to be greater than or equal to 3. So 51, 61, 71, 81, 91. So the next number 43 does not work because 4 − 3 is not greater or equal to 3. So 63, 73, 83, and 93. And then 75 doesn't work because 7 − 5 is not greater than or equal to 3. So 85, and 95 work.

(239) T: Go over how you got A to be 4, 5, 6, 7, 8, and 9. And go over how you got B to be 1 through 5.

(240) Kyle: O.K.

(241) T: Take it from the top.

(242) Kyle: O.K. B is only the odd numbers and it said that in the problem, so 1, 3, 5, 7, and 9. But it has to be less than or equal to 3 if you reverse it. So like if you have 75 and you reversed it you get 57 + 18 is not less than 75.

[T let Kyle go at this point.]

Although Kyle got the correct answer to the problem, it was not clear how he arrived at the answer based upon his explanations. If we examine his explanations carefully, we can find ambiguities, inconsistencies, and even some flawed logic. Kyle was right to begin with the condition for the solution since N is an odd number, the ones digit represented by B must be odd. But without making a mathematical argument or justification, he immediately jumped to the conclusion that B "is less than or equal to 5 or else it doesn't work." When told to go back and explain his logic again, Kyle used 7 as an example for B (judging from the context, what Kyle intended to say was that the next higher number than 5 and B could be is 7), and used 71 as an example for K. Doing so, Kyle was showing that if K was 71, then N would be 17, then 17 would not be greater than 71 + 18 (of course, one has to guess from his words to infer that he meant this).

The way Kyle proved his statement that B could not be greater than 5 was not convincing enough, because he used only one example to demonstrate that when B was 7 and A was 1 (i.e., N = 17) it did not work. What about other possibilities? Unless Kyle could show that all other possibilities (i.e., two-digit numbers) when B was greater than 5 did not work, his argument was prone to questioning. The teacher let Kyle go at this point. Kyle then made another statement about the tens digit without supporting argument or justification, that A is greater than or equal to 4 so that A was 4, 5, 6, 7, 8, and 9. Not only did Kyle not make an argument why A was greater than or equal to 4, he made a false statement about the relationship between A and B. Kyle stated that A − B has to be greater than or equal to B in the problem. Putting aside the problem of lacking an argument to support his statement, we can see that Kyle did not even notice the inconsistency between his statement about the relationship between A and B and the fact that in numbers 85 and 95 (two of the possible numbers for N), this relationship obviously did not hold and yet 85 and 95 still worked. Even worse, after Kyle finished his explanations, the teacher asked him to start all over again. Kyle gave very confusing explanations, "B is only the odd numbers and it said that in the problem, so 1, 3, 5, 7, and 9. But it has to be less than or equal to 3 if you reverse it. So like if you have 75 and you reversed it you get 57 + 18 is not less than 75." The last two sentences do not make any sense. Besides, it is ambiguous what has to be less than or equal to 3. Therefore, even though Kyle got the correct answer to the problem, we do not know how he arrived at the answer judging from his reasoning.

After Kyle finished, the teacher called Mike to present his solution, which read like this:

(243) Mike's solution:

$$N > K + 18$$
$$53 = 5(10) + 3$$
$$10t + u > 10u + t + 18$$
$$9t > 9u + 18$$
$$t > u + 2$$
$$u = 1, 2, 3, 4, 5, 6, 7, 8, 9$$
$$2 > \text{nothing will work}$$
$$3 > \text{nothing will work}$$
$$4 > 1 + 2$$
$$t = 4, 5, 6, 7, 8, 9$$
$$4 > 3$$
$$5 > 3 + 2 \text{ no}$$
$$5 > 1 + 2$$
$$5 > 3$$
$$6 > 1 + 2$$
$$6 > 1 + 3$$
$$7 > 1 + 2$$
$$7 > 3 + 2$$
$$7 > 5 + 2 \text{ no}$$
$$8 > 1 + 2$$
$$8 > 3 + 2$$
$$8 > 5 + 2$$
$$9 > 1 + 2$$
$$9 > 3 + 2$$
$$9 > 5 + 2$$

These would give you 41, 51, 61, 63, 71, 73, 81, 83, 85.

(244) Mike: Well, I separated it into the ten's and units and then like for 53, you can write 53, or you can write 5 times the 10's + the units. Because when you're flipping around the numbers, to get the two-digit number, 10 times the 10's digit + the unit is greater than switching this around. So you just multiply the units by 10 and the 10's is going to switch places. So like

9t> 9u + 18, so t > u + 2. So it connects to the tens, so 1, 2, 3, 4, 5, 6, 7, 8, 9. But N is odd, so it's not 2, 4, 6, 8. You can't start out with 1, 2, or 3. So let's say t is 2, the only way that this would work, it won't work. If you go to 3, it won't work. Because like if you had 30 and you switch the digits around to 03, it won't work. So 4 is greater than 1 + 2. So you start the tens with 4, 5, 6, 7, 8, and 9. So you plug in all these numbers. So then is 4 greater than 3? Yes, so the first number is 41. Is 4 greater than 3 + 2? No. So none of the other 4's work. So then we go to 5. Is 5 greater than 1 + 2? Yes. So 51 works. But that's the only 5 that works. So then go to 6. Is 6 greater than 1 + 2? Yes, so 61 works. So then is 6 greater than 3 + 2? Yes, so 63 works. So no other 6's will work. So 7, is it greater than 1 + 2? Yes, so 71 works, so 7 is greater than 3 + 2. That's all the 7's that work. So is 9 greater than 1 + 2? Yes, so 91 works. And 9 is greater than 3 + 2. So 9 is greater than 5 + 2. And that's it.

(245) B: What about the 8's?

(246) Mike: Oh, yeah. So is 8 greater than 1 + 2? Yes, so 81 works. So 8 is greater than 3 + 2, and 8 is greater than 5 + 2.

Compared to Kyle, Mike made an important advancement in his reasoning, using the idea of how two-digit numbers are formed and the condition given in the problem to establish an important relationship between the tens and ones digit (Mike used units instead of the ones digit), namely the tens digit must be greater than the ones digit plus 2 (i.e., t > u + 2). Mike also inferred that the ones unit (u) could not be 2, 4, 6, or 8 because N was an odd number. Instead of combining these pieces of information to make a mathematical argument of all the possibilities of N, Mike stated that, "You can't start out with 1, 2, or 3." Mike did not really make a rigorous case why one cannot start out with 1, 2, or 3 (in fact, using 30 was inconsistent with the condition that N was an odd number) and concluded that, "So you start the tens with 4, 5, 6, 7, 8, and 9." After this, Mike used the plug-in method to test different possibilities and found the answer. A third student, Chris, also presented his solution, which was the same as Mike's, but Chris was also unable to explain clearly why the tens unit has to be greater than 4. The teacher asked him why 4, and Chris simply used 3 as an example to show that it did not work. After that, Chris' logic became confusing and inconsistent:

(247) T: Why 4?

(248) Chris: Because when you put 3 in, it does not go, so it has to be greater than 4. So when you plug in 1, 3 isn't greater than 3, so 2 isn't greater than 3, so it has to be 4 − 10, and u has to be 1, 3, 5, 7, or 9.

(249) T: What is 4 − 10?

(250) Chris: 4 − 10 is t. No, it's 1 − 9 is t.

(251) T: O.K.

As can be seen, when Chris said, "1 − 9 is t," he was contradicting his earlier statement that t has to be greater than 4 (which is incorrect, since t can be 4). Moreover, Chris' conclusion that "u has to be 1, 3, 5, 7, or 9" not only was incorrect but also inconsistent with his final answer.

The three students' reasoning processes showed that even though these students could give the correct answer to the problem, none of them were able to make a clear, consistent, and logical mathematical argument about how they arrived at the correct answer. Moreover, the teacher did not capitalize on the errors to generate understanding with the group. Instead, the correct solution took precedence over the mathematical understanding. Although Mike and Chris were able to use the idea of how numbers are formed in the decimal system to establish the relationship between the tens and the ones digit in N (i.e., the tens digit must be greater than the ones digit plus 2, or alternatively, the tens digit minus the ones digit must be greater than 2), neither one exhibited an analytical ability (other than using the ambiguous plug-in method described by Mike and Chris) to connect this piece of information with the other information given in the problem (i.e., N is an odd number) to make an argument that the ones digit in N can only be 1, 3, or 5, whereas the corresponding tens digit would be {4,5,6,7,8,9}, {6,7,8,9}, and {8,9} respectively. This would give us all the possible two-digit numbers that N could be.

During these students' presentations, the teacher could have played a more active role than that we had observed, even though he asked them to clarify their reasoning at several places. When the students were unable to better explain their logic than what was already given, however, the teacher did not explore those areas where understanding was not evident. Moreover, once the presentations were over, the class was not given an opportunity to discuss and compare the solution methods presented to them. Therefore, we do not know if any of the ambiguous, inconsistent, or incorrect reasoning was taken as truth by the rest of the class. Importantly, an opportunity was lost for furthering the understanding of the concepts.

These classroom snapshots across grades and across levels indicate mathematics teaching and learning remains at the descriptive level. Teaching practices appear procedure driven with scant attention to conceptual understanding and problem solving. This is so, regardless of whether the mathematics topics were two-digit or multi-digit subtractions with regrouping, or Algebra. All topics were essentially reduced to basic arithmetic manipulation.

NINE HUNDRED OBSERVATIONS: NO TEACHING FOR MATHEMATICAL UNDERSTANDING

One point worth mentioning is that the discourse of mathematics teaching and learning depicted through these snapshots consistently characterizes mathematics lessons contained in over 900 classroom observations. Chapter 1 described one elementary teacher who was reviewing and teaching her 2nd graders the concept of probability through experiment following the textbook. Although the textbook's idea of teaching the concept of probability through experiment was a good one, whether students were able to understand the concept or not ultimately depended on the teacher's understanding of the concept, particularly when students were confused by the seemingly inconsistent experiment result and what they had learned about the concept of probability.

Relying on textbooks alone, therefore, will not bring out teaching for understanding, which requires a deep understanding of: (1) the mathematical topics and ideas in the textbook; (2) the connection between different mathematical topics and ideas; and (3) the pedagogies that are helpful for student understanding. Such an understanding can arise only from careful studying of and thinking about the materials in the textbook. Simply going through the procedures or steps in the textbook will not solve the problem of students' lack of understanding of materials presented to them. The treatment of topics such as place value, regrouping, and two-digit subtraction with regrouping in the teachers' manual revealed that the textbook made an attempt to emphasize the connection among these mathematical concepts and the importance of helping students understand the concept of place value. However, such information may be useless if teachers do not recognize its significance or do not have the time and energy for a careful study of manuals.

NOTES

1. Where names are used, they are pseudonyms. Notations are as follows: T-teacher, S-a student, Ss-students, T/Ss- teacher and students together, B-boy, G-girl, H-Hispanic, BH-Hispanic boy, and GH-Hispanic girl.
2. The teacher said 5's, not 1's and never corrected her misstatement or student's misunderstanding.

REFERENCES

Ma, L. (1999). *Knowing and teaching elementary mathematics: Teachers' understanding of fundamental mathematics in China and the United States* (1st ed.). Mahwah: Lawrence Erlbaum Associates, Inc.

Ma, L. (2010). *Knowing and teaching elementary mathematics: Teachers' understanding of fundamental mathematics in China and the United States* (2nd ed.). New York: Routledge.

Wu, H. H. (2011). *Understanding numbers in elementary school mathematics.* Providence: American Mathematical Society.

CHAPTER 3

Teachers' and Math Coaches' Understanding of Basic Mathematical Ideas

In Chap. 2, extensive qualitative analyses summarized the discourse in classrooms addressing the concept of place value in grades 2, 4, 8, and 10. The analyses documented how teachers followed a discourse norm that focused on procedural knowledge and failed to create opportunities to learn mathematical concepts. As a result, students were unable to construct mathematically valid arguments even in honors classes in the upper grades. Qualitative analysis of classroom teaching and learning in Chap. 2 also showed that students at these upper grades did not have a solid grasp of the concept of place value that should have been addressed beginning in early grades.

Part of the explanations for why students are not provided with opportunities to learn mathematics concepts could be the mathematical understanding of teachers. Based on cross-cultural analysis of two groups of elementary teachers' understanding of four standard mathematical topics between China and the USA, Liping Ma suggested two reasons for why Chinese students outperform US students (1999, 2010). These two factors are: (1) Chinese teachers begin their teaching careers with a better understanding of elementary mathematics than that of most US elementary teachers; and (2) Chinese teachers' understanding of the mathematics they teach continues to grow throughout their professional lives. Chapters 3, 4, and 5 focus on these two critical issues by examining key system actors' mathematical understanding (i.e., elementary and secondary teachers, and mathematics coaches), pre-service mathematics teachers' content understanding and

© The Author(s) 2018
X. A. Newton, *Improving Teacher Knowledge in K-12 Schooling*,
https://doi.org/10.1007/978-3-319-71207-9_3

training (undergraduate STEM majors), and in-service teachers' professional development opportunities to grow mathematically, respectively.

Specifically, this chapter presents elementary and secondary teachers' responses to two teaching scenario questions aimed at probing their understanding of two mathematics topics that involve understanding the concept of place value. The two topics are two-digit subtraction with regrouping and multi-digit multiplication. These two topics represent two standard topics in elementary mathematics. The two topics were purposely chosen because they could provide us with a glimpse of respondents' understanding of a basic mathematical concept (i.e., place value) and its application in these two common mathematical topics.

In addition to teachers, mathematics coaches were also asked the 2-digit subtraction with regrouping question. Coaching is considered as one of the key professional development strategies for promoting effective instruction and student achievement (Elmore 2002; Fenstermacher 1985; Kohler et al. 1997). Consequently, it is important to know whether coaches are equipped with the kind of mathematical understanding that will enable them to support teachers' continuous development of an in-depth understanding of mathematical content knowledge.

The purpose of this chapter is to emphasize the point that as simple as K-12 mathematical topics may seem to be on the surface, the depth of understanding that is required in order to teach these topics effectively (or teach them well) is not as superficial as we may think. In the sections that follow, analysis of teachers' responses is presented first, followed by results for the mathematics coaches.

ELEMENTARY TEACHERS' RESPONSES

The scenario question[1] used to tap elementary teachers' understanding of the concept of place value and its application in two-digit subtraction with regrouping is as follows:

> In this section, let's spend some time thinking about one particular topic that you may work with when you teach, subtraction with regrouping. Let's take a look at these two problems:
>
> $$52 \qquad 91$$
> $$\underline{-25} \quad \underline{-79}$$

How would you approach these problems if you were teaching 2nd grade? What, would you say, students need to understand or be able to do before they could start learning subtraction with regrouping?

WHAT WAS THE FOCUS OF TEACHERS' RESPONSES?

When asked how they would approach those two problems (i.e., subtraction with regrouping), teachers tended to focus on the procedural or computational aspects rather than conceptual understanding of the problem. Teachers' explanations typically resembled the following responses:

T1:   And thinking back on how I taught it, just basically some of the steps that I would lead them through would be, first always remember that you start on the right-hand side of the problem, that's the side that your pencil's in if you're right handed, in the ones column. And then ask yourself do you have—does the ones column number have enough or do you have to, and if it doesn't have enough then he's going to have to borrow from his neighbor, from the five or the tens column, and what do you do, what are the steps? You cross out the 5, you make it one smaller, what number do you always give to the ones column: You always give a one to the one column and then you subtract 12 minus 5, you could use your fingers, draw a line, 12 minus 5 is 7 and 5 became a 4, 4 minus 2 is 2. And that's basically the steps that I lead them through there to get the answer.

T2:   Well first thing I'd do is have students make sure that the tens are under the tens, the ones are under the ones and then we start with the ones and I teach them the chant that they have to say. They have to first look at the ones, if the bottom number is bigger than the top number you have to regroup then I tell them go over and ask Mr. Five, well Mr. Five can I borrow one of your tens and they say yes how many will you leave me, at that point in time they need to cross out the 2 and make it 12 then they can subtract 12 take away 5 is 7 and 4 take away 2 is 2. And same thing with the other problems, always look at the ones who—we say that chant 2 or 3 times at least every day to remind them.

T3:   If I was teaching second grade I would probably use base ten blocks first, I would put ten, the 5 tens and 2 ones and 2 tens and 5 ones and then I would definitely use for one of the 5 tens I would have one that would break apart so we could change it into the ones and show them how to take one of the tens and bring it over the ones place and then how they can take 5 away from that and then the 4 tens would be left and take 2 tens away.

While these responses, typical of the teachers we interviewed, may seem very different on the surface, they were actually quite similar in terms of the focus of teaching and learning. As can be seen from teacher 1's (T1's) response, the focus of the teaching was on the procedure of computing, "You cross out the 5, you make it one smaller, what number do you always give to the ones column: You always give a one to the one column and then you subtract 12 minus 5, you could use your fingers, draw a line, 12 minus 5 is 7 and 5 became a 4, 4 minus 2 is 2." The way of teaching described as such does not at all explain why it is necessary to regroup.

Similarly, teacher 2 (T2) focused on the steps that the children must take: "make sure that the tens are under the tens, the ones are under the ones," "look at the ones," "you have to regroup," and "cross out the 2 and make it 12 then they can subtract." Note that the teacher prescribed *actions*—look, regroup, cross out, subtract—for the child to complete in order to solve the problem. In a similar way the third teacher's (T3) response described a procedure of actions: "I would use," "I would put," "we could change," "take one of the tens," "bring it over," "take 5 away," and "take 2 tens away." This dictation of action approach is indicative of a procedural model of learning that addresses *how* to regroup but does not explain conceptually *why* regrouping is necessary in the first place. Knowing *why* holds the key to understanding and solving subtraction with regrouping in all contexts (i.e., two-digit, three-digit, and so on).

Though the manipulatives employed by teacher 3 (T3) in theory have the potential to lend to conceptual development (and may in fact help), the teacher here is merely "show[ing] them *how*" to use the manipulatives in the same way that the other two teachers show the students *how* to do the arithmetic operation on paper. Neither method explicitly addresses *why* the regrouping is necessary.

WHY WAS THERE A NEED TO REGROUP?

When describing the need for regrouping in solving the two problems, teachers tended to give oversimplified, underdeveloped, or even mathematically problematic explanations. One of the popular expressions, as stated in the previous response (see T1), was that "[D]oes the ones column have enough, and if it doesn't have enough then he's going to have to borrow from his neighbor, from the five or the tens column." This sentiment (i.e., not enough ones) is echoed by teacher 4's (T4's) response shown below:

T4:   We would see that if they have two [ones] that they don't have enough to take 5 away, so then they would need to borrow more, and then so where would they borrow, they would borrow from the 10's.

The teacher's explanation that "if it (i.e., the ones digit) doesn't have enough then he's going to have to borrow from his neighbor, from the five or the tens column" is treating the two digits as independent numbers that are not related to each other, which does not convey any real mathematical meaning.

Furthermore, the statement that "they don't have enough [ones]" is not entirely accurate, as there are plenty of ones (that are composed into higher place value units). The notion of "borrowing" from the 10's separates the digits and treats them as distinct numbers when in fact they are, as a whole, the representation of a single number. Attention to such details is important when teaching young students, because only an accurate and well-developed understanding will establish the solid conceptual foundation that is necessary for students' future mathematical conceptual development.

Another statement that teachers frequently made was that one cannot subtract a bigger number from a smaller one and use this as a rationale for the need to regroup in subtraction problems like $52 - 25$. As one teacher put it:

T5:   I guess you have to keep reminding them that you can't subtract a big number from a small number. I know that even my third graders they keep forgetting that if you have a small number you can't take away a bigger number. So I keep telling them if you only have two pencils, could I take five away from you? I have to keep reminding them about the borrowing part.

T6:   Well first of all you have to start at the one's place and you cannot subtract 5 from 2 because 2 is smaller and on the second problem 1 is smaller than 9 so then they have to regroup.

The teacher's statement (T5) that "you can't subtract a big number from a small number" is inconsistent with the two problems that are presented in the interview question (i.e., 52 − 25 and 91 − 79). In both problems, we are subtracting a smaller number from a bigger one (i.e., 25 is smaller than 52 and 79 is smaller than 91). Therefore, rather than helping students to see that it makes perfect sense to take a number in the twenties away from a number in the fifties, the teacher made a statement that is inconsistent with the problem.

Moreover, the teacher's statement (T5) that "you can't subtract a big number from a small number" or "if you have a small number you can't take away a bigger number" is mathematically problematic. Subtracting a bigger number from a smaller one is a mathematically valid operation, which students will learn at later grades. Even though at 2nd grade students are not able to do such operations, they should not be confused by teachers' inaccurate statements that might affect their future mathematics learning.

The phrase "you cannot subtract 5 from 2" (see T6) was a popular but mathematically incorrect response. An accurate explanation would state that two minus five is a mathematically valid operation which 2nd graders have not yet been taught. Among the 80 plus elementary teachers who provided their responses, only a couple of them made this distinction.

How Would Teachers Normally Teach This Topic?

Since teachers tended to focus on the procedural or computational aspects of the mathematics problems presented in the scenario, their approach to teaching put emphasis on teacher demonstration and student drill and practice. In other words, the methods teachers use to help students with the problem do not focus on an understanding of the concept, but rather on pushing students to remember the mechanical procedures of computation. For instance, some teachers mentioned drawing a line down the middle between the ones and the tens digit. As one teacher put it:

> I'd write it on the board and just start with the ones column. Usually what I'll do is I'll draw a line down the middle between the ones and the tens to show that, and use different colors to show them that you need to do each column separately and one at a time.

The strategies that teachers employed tended to focus on computational skills to train students for current arithmetic demands rather than on conceptual understanding. About 37% of teachers described teaching strategies that were purely computational in focus. These responses were typically as follows:

Well once they establish a foundation of being able to add and subtract up to 18 [which] they need before they could begin regrouping, once they could do that first thing [what] I would do would be to start with the ones column, borrow from your neighbor if you don't have enough, cross out your neighbor, make him one smaller, give a one to the number that's borrowing so the 2 would become a 12 and 52 – 25, 12 – 7's 5 [note the teacher made an error here because the problem is 52 – 25; not 52 – 27], the 5 became a 4 because you gave one to his neighbor, 4 – 2 is 2, that's how I basically teach it.

Some of these teachers made up rhymes or stories, such as "I have this little mnemonic device, BBB, bottom bigger borrow" or "First of all, I would turn it into a little story. So, once upon a time there was a girl who had fifty-two Barbie dolls...." Even with these devices, the focus here was still purely on computation. The rhyme or stories merely aided in helping students remember steps to carry out the arithmetic operation.

Other teachers tried to come up with tricks to help students. As one teacher said:

Well, the first thing that comes to mind is some kind of trick that will help them to remember to be careful in the basic functions of doing the processes involved. There're a lot of different processes here. First they have to recognize that it's a minus sign and not a plus sign, which sounds simple but a lot of children they just do what they are more comfortable with, [and] they're more comfortable with addition. So quite often many children will just add everything they see. So I would go through a lot of drills on focusing in on the signs. Then the next thing I would really focus in on is the fact that you need to regroup in both of these problems. So I have a little poem I drill into their heads from the first day. It goes, the bottom bigger borrow, the bottom bigger borrow. I know borrow isn't a popular word right now, but I've been teaching a long time and it's hard to get that out of my vocabulary. I say it, bottom bigger borrow, bottom bigger borrow. It drills it into their heads and they think it's funny. They love to say bottom bigger borrow. So they're always looking for an opportunity to say, bottom bigger borrow, and it's something that helps. It will remind them to pay attention to the place value and to do the regrouping that they have already been taught to do.

Another teacher thought of using a rhyme to help students:

> Now, how I like to teach it is we start with a rhyme called More On Top, No Need to Stop. That means they don't need to regroup. This second, more on the floor, here's the floor, go next door, get 10 more. Number's the same, zero's the game. If they get that rhyme, they should be able to understand this.

A few teachers mentioned using manipulatives, typically base ten blocks, to teach subtraction with regrouping in order to make it more concrete rather than abstract to students. As one teacher described:

> I would start out by using base ten blocks so that could review the place value and that you start subtracting always with the ones. You have two ones, you need to subtract 5, they can see then with the blocks they don't have enough ones they just have the two, because they represented 52 in the model. So they would need to regroup, which means they would take that ten block away and exchange it for 10 ones, which they would put with the two they already have. Then they can take away or subtract 5 and see that there were 7 blocks. Then over to the tens column you can <inaudible> and they would have the 4 tens left, they would physically again take away the two and see that there are two left.

Although the idea of easing students' understanding through using manipulatives is a good one, the way it is used as described by the teacher suggests that its use really focuses on the steps of calculation rather than on helping students to understand the mathematical reasoning or the concept underlying the steps.

Some teachers mentioned using manipulatives to "teaching conceptually", but the way that manipulatives were employed as these teachers described indicated that the end goal was still computational proficiency rather than conceptual understanding. Methods for using manipulatives were typically stated as follows:

> Second grade I would probably use base ten blocks to start with and you know, when you regroup from the tens place I would show them how you could convert that into ten ones. So I think I would teach it conceptually that way first and then, you know, just get into the standard procedures for doing it.

Clearly, manipulatives are being used as an on-ramp for computation. The ultimate goal is developing computational skills rather than conceptual understanding.

Perhaps the best example that showed teachers' emphasis on procedural or computational skills instead of conceptual understanding was when they created procedural steps or strategies to address a conceptual problem. For instance, it is not an uncommon practice for 2nd graders to attempt to take 2 in the subtrahend (i.e., 52) from 5 in the minuend (25), instead of the other way around. Teachers were aware of such a common error and assumed it to be computational, as evidenced in the way they addressed the problem:

> A lot of children become confused and they might try to subtract five minus two instead of two minus five... reminding kids [that] if the bottom's bigger that you have to borrow, having little catch phrases like that will help them so they don't subtract [the other way around]. You know, 2 take away 5 isn't 3 [in this situation].

Students who did such subtraction demonstrated a lack of conceptual understanding. The remedy for this lack of understanding as presented by the teacher was creating a procedural checkpoint ("if the bottom's bigger that you have to borrow"), instead of helping students understand what was going on when we conduct subtraction with regrouping.

None of the teachers in the sample were able to explain clearly the importance of helping students to understand the concept of place value, as evidenced in the following response given by a Chinese elementary teacher (Ma 1999, 2010):

> What is the rate for composing a higher value unit? The answer is simple: 10. Ask students how many ones there are in a 10, or ask them what the rate for composing a higher value unit is, their answers will be the same: 10. However, the effect of the two questions on their learning is not the same. When you remind students that 1 ten equals 10 ones, you tell them the fact that is used in the procedure. And, this somehow confines them to the fact. *When you require them to think about the rate for composing a higher value unit, you lead them to a theory that explains the fact as well as the procedure.* Such an understanding is more powerful than a specific fact. It can be applied to more situations. Once they realize that the rate of composing a higher value unit, 10, is the reason why we decompose a ten into 10 ones, they will apply it to other situations. You don't need to remind them again

that 1 hundred equals 10 tens when in the future they learn subtraction with three-digit numbers. They will be able to figure it out on their own. (Ma 1999, pp. 10–11)

This Chinese teacher's development of the concept of place value in terms of a rate of composition creates a lesson that focuses on the long-term conceptual development of the students. Conversely, none of the teachers we studied articulated such a well-developed concept of place value (i.e., as a rate of composition); instead their lessons focused on short-term arithmetical development (see Chap. 2). An underdeveloped conceptualization of the content is associated then with a short-sighted pedagogy, namely, a pedagogy that fails to place students' future conceptual development at the focus of instruction.

Secondary Math Teachers' Responses

Secondary math teachers were asked to respond to the following scenario question:[2]

Some eighth-grade teachers noticed that several of their students were making the same mistake in multiplying large numbers. In trying to calculate:

$$\begin{array}{r} 123 \\ \times 645 \\ \hline \end{array}$$

the students seemed to be forgetting to "move the numbers" (i.e., the partial products) over on each line. They were doing this:

$$\begin{array}{r} 123 \\ \times 645 \\ \hline 615 \\ 492 \\ 738 \\ \hline 1845 \end{array}$$

instead of this:

$$123$$
$$\times 645$$
$$615$$
$$492$$
$$\underline{738}$$
$$79{,}335$$

While these teachers agreed that this stacking was a problem, they did not agree on what to do about it. What would you do if you were teaching 8th grade and you noticed that several of your students were doing this?

What Was Teachers' Interpretation of Why Students Made Errors?

Teachers who are procedurally oriented interpreted students' mistake as merely a problem of lining the numbers up, as one teacher said, "But the problem is lining them up. And so what we leave as commonly as spaces here are actually zeros." The remedy therefore focuses on the stacking or lining up of numbers, as one teacher described:

> If I noticed that they are forgetting about stacking, then [I would] recommend to add zeros, because sometimes they forget about leaving one space for every digit. So they can use zeros instead of spaces.

Though the phrase "leaving one space for every digit" seemed to refer to the concept of place value, the interpretation as a whole focused on the *location* of the numbers (i.e., place rather than *value*). Interpretations such as this missed the correct representation of the fundamental concept, place value.

Around 45% of the 80 plus teachers pointed out the need for students to understand the importance of place value, and yet wound up giving similar responses. As one teacher described:

> I would break down the problem to get the concept across to them that I'm not multiplying by one, but I'm multiplying by 100, I'm not multiplying by

two but I'm multiplying by 20 and so on. I'd set up the three different problems that would present me with my zeros, moving my spaces over and then have them get the three products that they've gotten.

Some teachers, though using the term "place value", focused on the location of the numbers (i.e., place rather than value). As one teacher put it:

> Well I would explain that each line has to go over on because of the place value that needs to be the right place value. Like in the ten's place, the hundred's place.

This response is essentially the same as the one given by another teacher:

> I'd explain to them that you do the series of moving from your right to your left and each time you move to another number you would move one space over to the left.

These interpretations, regardless of the format of the response, missed the correct representation of the fundamental concept, place value. On the surface, we might think that this teacher had a conceptual focus ("I would break down the problem to get the concept across to them that I'm not multiplying by one, but I'm multiplying by 100"). The teacher pointed out that the 1 in the hundreds place was not 1 but 100. The teacher, however, did not follow the conceptual direction one might expect from the second part of the statement (i.e., "would present me with my zeros, moving my spaces over"). The focus was on *how* to move over the numbers, not *why*. In other words, the attention was on the *location*, instead of the *value* of the partial products. The emphasis, therefore, was still reinforcing the procedural aspect (i.e., lining up the numbers) of the operation.

Several teachers attempted to explain the rationale for the mistake as a lack of understanding of the concept of place value on the part of students. As one teacher explained:

> Basically I would explain that when you're multiplying 123 times 645 they have to understand place value, place value's the key. The 3 and the 5 represent the ones column and 3 times 5 is 15 but the 2 and the 4 represent ten, 2 isn't really 2 it's 20 and 4 is 40. So they need to understand that 5 times 2 may be 10 but 5 times 20 is 100. So that's why we have to add the zeros. And the shortcut that you would teach them is [that with] the first place value you just bring the number straight down. Every time you move one place to the left you add another zero underneath so if you're multiplying from the third place there have to be two zeros under the 4 and 5 for that place value because 6 really represents 600 not 6.

This teacher pointed out that the understanding of place value is the key to solving the problem correctly. The teacher further explained that the value of 2 in 123 or 4 in 645 is different from the value of 3 in 123 or 5 in 645, because 2 is really 20 and 4 is really 40. And that is "why we have to add the zeros." The focus on the rationale is definitely an advance over the emphasis on the procedure of lining numbers up. After trying to explain where the zeros come, however, the teacher described the way to teach students as a set of rules:

> And the shortcut that you would teach them is [that with] the first place value you just bring the number straight down. Every time you move one place to the left you add another zero underneath so if you're multiplying from the third place there have to be two zeros under the 4 and 5 for that place value because 6 really represents 600 not 6.

What Were Teachers' Teaching Strategies?

As described in the previous responses, one of the ways that teachers approach the problem is through stipulating rules or procedures, as represented in the following response:

> I'd just advise them of the rule. And the first one, 123 times 5, they are aware of that one. Because that's not where the mistake is. You've seen this before, so I don't think I need to point to it. You just want to get my response. This is just units, so this is literally 5 times 123, and then I want to make them aware that when they get to the second line, that's not 123 times 4, that's 123 times 40. And I think if they're aware it's 123 times 40, you know, they should have an understanding of why they're moving when they get to the second line. Why they're moving beyond the units place. And then the same thing when I do the last one, 123 times 6. I want them to know that it's not 123 times 6, it's 123 times 600. And hopefully they'll know that's why they're skipping the two places there.

The teachers also suggested breaking down the problem and going through it step by step until students arrived at the correct solution:

> I would tell the students to multiply 123 times 5 separately then multiply again 123 times 4, like a different problem and then finally multiply as a third problem 123 times 6. Once we get the answers then we'll bring them together as one, noting that you start your answer under the number, that's where we line them up.

Although these teachers tended to focus on describing the rules, they at least paid attention to explaining the rationale for why zeros were there by alluding to the concept of place value. Other teachers focused exclusively on the computational procedures and means to force students to move "the numbers over" and to "line the number up." Typical methods these teachers frequently used include using lined paper or placeholders such as "0" or "X."

For instance, one teacher described the use of graph paper, "First of all I would use graphing paper. That would be one idea to get them to line up." Other methods teachers frequently used to force students to "line the numbers up" include using lined paper or placeholders such as "0:"

> What I would probably do is placeholder. In other words, I would teach them after the first line put a placeholder as a zero for the next number. So, since it's the second line you're going to put one placeholder and then when you go to the third line, you're going to put two placeholders, so you're going to put two zeros. That way they know automatically that they're going to have a total of three zeros because they're multiplying by three numbers. So, that's what I would tell them to do. That way they don't forget.

Which is similar to using "X" as a placeholder:

> Well I'd go over several examples of the correct method. Then what I'd do, as you shift over, and have them maybe put an X in there to take up the place value for it. And maybe that would help solve the problem. The first one has an X, the second one has two X's, the third one has three X's and they'd just continue with that format.

As discussed previously, even when teachers tried to focus on the concept of place value, they had the tendency to prescribe the rules for students rather than helping them to understand the algorithm by presenting a rigorous argument, as exhibited in the following example from another Chinese elementary teacher (Ma 1999, 2010):

> The problem is that the student did not have a clear idea of why the numbers should be lined up in the way seemingly different from that in addition. The lining up is actually derived through several steps. First, I will put on the board an equation and work it through with students:

$$123 \times 645 = 123 \times (600 + 40 + 5)$$
$$= 123 \times 600 + 123 \times 40 + 123 \times 5$$
$$= 73800 + 4920 + 615$$
$$= 78720 + 615$$
$$= 79335$$

What allowed us to transform the problem? The distributive law. Then, I will suggest that the class rewrite the equation into columns:

$$
\begin{array}{r}
123 \\
\times 645 \\
\hline
615 \\
4920 \\
\underline{73800} \\
79{,}335
\end{array}
$$

I will ask students to observe the zeros in the equation as well as those in the columns. Do they affect the sum? Why yes, and why no? Can the zeros in the equation be eliminated? How about the zeros in the columns? If we erase the zeros in the columns, what will happen? Then I will erase the zeros in the columns and we will get staircase-like columns on the board:

$$
\begin{array}{r}
123 \\
\times 645 \\
\hline
615 \\
492 \\
\underline{738} \\
79{,}335
\end{array}
$$

After such a discussion I believe that the lining-up way in multiplication will make sense to the students, and also, become impressive to them. (Ma 1999, pp. 40–41)

Compared to the responses that teachers in our sample provided, this Chinese teacher's response is closer to a conventional mathematical argument with features of justification, rigorous reasoning, and correct expression.

MATHEMATICS COACHES' RESPONSES

The mathematics coaches (both elementary and secondary)[3] were asked the following question:

In this section, let's spend some time thinking about one particular topic that you may work with when you teach subtraction with regrouping. Let's take a look at these two problems:

$$
\begin{array}{cc}
52 & 91 \\
-25 & -79 \\
\hline
\end{array}
$$

How would you approach these problems if you were teaching the 2nd grade?

WHAT WAS THE FOCUS OF ELEMENTARY COACHES' RESPONSES?

Coaches, as a group, did not give a conceptually focused response as demonstrated by the Chinese teacher. Most coaches (72%) gave pseudo-conceptual responses—responses that seemed conceptually focused but upon closer inspection were actually procedurally focused answers with an exhibition of conceptual activities or rhetoric. The following is one such response from a coach:

> They can show me what a 53 looks like using the objects. And now we're going to take away 27, so we go through like a whole acting kind of thing where I am the banker, I'm the person with the extra pieces, and the students can hand me this exchange for 10 unit pieces, and then the student needs to put those unit pieces over here. And so we go through this many many times without even looking at the algorithms, until I feel absolutely satisfied that they can do it with concrete objects. Then we start building in

the algorithms, but even then I will have students typically solve that 53 and we're going to take away 27, solve it first with the objects and then tell me, "Okay explain to me how you did that. Okay, and we'll put it here," and I have the student explain to me exactly how they did that. I had to take 7 ones away but I only had 3 ones in the ones place, to I went over to the tens place and I took away a 10 and I exchanged that for 10 ones, so now I have 13 ones, but I only have 4 tens. And then I subtracted starting in the ones place or whatever. So typically that's how I'd teach it.

Though this coach insisted on using manipulatives, the goal was for students to be able to "do it [subtraction] with concrete objects." The focus was still on being able to carry out a procedure, only this time it was with objects rather than on paper. The learning resulting from this way of teaching would not be significantly different from that resulting from a strictly procedural approach to teaching without using any manipulatives.

Why Was There a Need to Regroup?

The fact that coaches gave even less explanation than teachers as to why there was a need to regroup further illustrated a lack of conceptual focus. Seventy-two percent of the coaches gave vague reasoning or no explanation at all as to why regrouping was necessary. The remaining 28% of coaches typically gave the same problematic responses as seen in the teachers' responses.

How Would Coaches Normally Teach This Topic?

Only one coach (out of 18 elementary mathematics coaches) used purely procedural strategies (as opposed to 37% of teachers) while most coaches (83%) used the same pseudo-conceptual strategies. Two coaches however, attempted to give a more conceptual-based strategy for teaching:

So we might talk about simply thinking that maybe 52 we could break it into tens and ones and maybe we would call it 50 plus 2. And then we might decide well what would happen if we took—if we decided to break it down another way, and maybe someone would say, 40 plus 12. And then we would look at 25 and we could break that up into tens and ones, and maybe we would say it was 20 plus 5. And we would know that we're talking about the same number, but we're just calling it something else. And we'd have to remember what the sign meant because we've got some plus signs here. So we might put parentheses around it to help us remember....So maybe we'll put a square or a rectangle around it because we have to know that things are going to get smaller. And then we know that we can start it either way. We can do it with the ones or we can do it with the tens. It doesn't really matter. You want to start with the tens, we can, and we know that we have 40 and we know if we minus 20 we know we have 20, and then we know if we have 12, and we are taking 5 away, and now we have 7. And then we have to remember we're dealing with both and doing both together.

Proposing different ways of representing the number 52 (i.e., 40 plus 12, or 50 plus 2) is an advance. However, the coach's statement that "we can start it either way...It doesn't really matter" can be limiting when students learn higher-digit (e.g., three-digit, four-digit, and so on) subtraction with regrouping. The approach proposed by this coach was still to teach a method (i.e., to rewrite the numbers in a different format, 40 + 12) rather than the underlying principle of how numbers are formed in the decimal system and its application in subtraction with regrouping.

WHAT WAS THE FOCUS OF THE SECONDARY COACHES' RESPONSES?

Similarly, secondary mathematics coaches tended to focus on the procedures for solving the problem, rather than the conceptual understanding of the problem. Within these procedural answers, the coaches were split as to how they would go about demonstrating the procedures. Forty-seven percent of the coaches (out of 16 secondary coaches) said that they would use some type of manipulative, while 53% said they would demonstrate the procedures in a straightforward manner. Mostly, the coaches gave very simplistic responses and did not explain why regrouping was necessary and their responses tended to focus on "showing" their students' steps, instead of explaining the mathematical concept behind the computation.

NOTES

1. This scenario question was used by Liping Ma (1999, p. 1) in her investigation of Chinese and American teachers' understanding of elementary mathematics topics.
2. This question was adapted from the question that Liping Ma (1999, p. 28) used to investigate Chinese and American teachers' understanding of elementary mathematics topics.
3. Eighteen elementary and 16 secondary.

REFERENCES

Elmore, R. F. (2002). *Bridging the gap between standards and achievement: The imperative for professional development in education.* Washington, DC: The Albert Shanker Institute.

Fenstermacher, G. D. (1985). Determining the value of staff development. *The Elementary School Journal, 85*(3), 281–314.

Kohler, F. W., Crilley, K. M., Shearer, D. D., & Good, G. (1997). Effects of peer coaching on teacher and student outcomes. *Journal of Educational Research, 90*(4), 240–251.

Ma, L. (1999). *Knowing and teaching elementary mathematics: Teachers' understanding of fundamental mathematics in China and the United States.* Mahwah: Lawrence Erlbaum Associates.

Ma, L. (2010). *Knowing and teaching elementary mathematics: Teachers' understanding of fundamental mathematics in China and the United States* (2nd ed.). New York: Routledge.

CHAPTER 4

Undergraduate STEM Majors' Understanding of Slope

Data in Chap. 3 shows teachers' and mathematics coaches' understanding of foundational mathematical topics is fragile (i.e., two-digit subtraction with regrouping and multi-digit multiplication). As a platform for addressing mathematics teachers' content understanding, this chapter explores this issue further by investigating a group of undergraduate STEM majors' understanding of a foundational algebra concept, slope, based on the Common Core Mathematics Standards (CCMS). CCMS is a major effort at revamping the US K-12 mathematics education in order to improve American students' mathematical performance and international competitiveness. To ensure the successful implementation of CCMS, there have been calls for both recruiting from those with the strongest quantitative backgrounds (e.g., STEM majors) and offering rigorous mathematics training in teacher preparation (Schmidt et al. 2011). Missing from the discourse are questions of whether STEM majors, who arguably represent the strongest candidates for the teaching force, have the depth of content understanding in order to teach mathematical topics at the rigorous level that CCMS expects, and whether future mathematics teachers need the opportunities to learn rigorously the K-12 mathematical topics they are expected to teach down the road.

This chapter addresses the knowledge gap in these two areas through investigating the understanding of the concept of slope among a group STEM majors who were enrolled in an undergraduate experimental teacher preparation program. This program offers a unique opportunity to

© The Author(s) 2018   75
X. A. Newton, *Improving Teacher Knowledge in K-12 Schooling*,
https://doi.org/10.1007/978-3-319-71207-9_4

examine the mathematical understanding of prospective teachers, because the mathematics department offers a three-course sequence coursework focusing on grades 6 through 12 mathematics topics for mathematics majors who intend to pursue teaching as a career. The content of these courses aligns well with the CCMS, which enables us to assess if there is any qualitative difference in the understanding of the slope concept between those who took the course versus those who did not.

Data suggest that even among these students there are gaps in their conceptual understanding of slope and of the connection between a linear equation and its graph. These weaknesses could pose challenges for their preparedness to teach the slope concept consistent with the rigor that CCMS calls for. Taking courses that specifically address the K-12 mathematics topics is helpful. The chapter discusses the implications of these findings for the content preparation of mathematics teachers.

Scenario Question Assessing STEM Majors' Understanding of Slope

The following scenario question was used to investigate pre-service STEM majors' understanding of the concept of slope and the connection between a linear equation and its graph:

How would you help *eighth graders* understand that the slope of a non-vertical line can be calculated using any two distinct points on the line (e.g., the slope of the line below can be calculated with points P_1 and P_2 or points P_3 and P_4)?

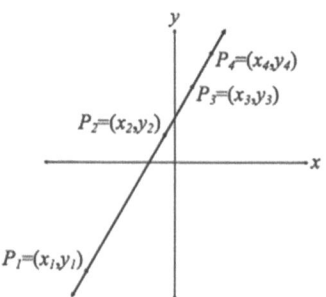

Before presenting findings on what study participants' responses reveal about their understanding of slope, it is important to know why the slope concept provides an ideal platform for investigating the question of whether teacher candidates are adequately prepared to teach mathematics at the level of rigor that is required by CCMS.

Why Slope?

The concept of slope occupies a significant part of the early algebra curriculum and has wide applications in real-world problems (e.g., studying the relationship between supply/demand and the price of goods in economics) and is foundational for studying more advanced mathematical topics such as functions (and functions are important for many science disciplines). Despite its importance, research has well documented the difficulties both students and teachers (pre- and in-service) have in terms of understanding the concept of slope (Stump 2001a, b; Teuscher and Reys 2010; Zaslavsky et al. 2002). This difficulty will likely increase with the adoption of CCMS, because it approaches the concept of slope in significantly different ways.

To begin with, CCMS makes the distinction between the slope of a line and the slope of two chosen points on the line. In contrast, most existing textbooks conflate the two. Furthermore, CCMS emphasizes reasoning and proof. Therefore, CCMS requires that students be able to prove that the slope of a line can be defined by *any* two distinctive points on the line. The proof invokes the concept of similar triangles and therefore, according to CCMS, students will be exposed to the concept of similar triangles before learning the concept of slope. This also means that students are expected to have a much stronger grasp of the connection between linear equations and their graphs than was expected in the past. This logical sequence of topics and the emphasis on the connection between equations and graphs are absent in the current curriculum and textbooks (Wu 2014) and signals the significant departure of CCMS from the old ways of teaching and learning of slope (Schmidt and Houang 2012).

What Is Slope? Review of State Standards, Textbooks, and Research

Considerable research has been conducted on the topic of slope and has documented extensively the difficulties students (Barr 1980, 1981; Greenes et al. 2007; Hauger 1997; Leinhardt et al. 1990; Lobato 1996,

2008; Lobato and Siebert 2002; Lobato and Thanheiser 1999, 2002; Postelnicu 2011; Stump 2001b; Teuscher and Reys 2010; Zaslavsky et al. 2002), pre-service teacher candidates (Stump 2001a; Zaslavsky et al. 2002), and in-service teachers (Stump 1996, 1997, 1999; Zaslavsky et al. 2002) had encountered in terms of understanding the concept of slope. The vast difficulty with the concept of slope might be due to many factors, although it is not clear from the literature which factors matter the most. This chapter focuses on how slope is typically defined (or conceptualized) in the research literature, by state standards and different textbooks, because these are the key resources for people to learn what slope is. The definition or conceptualization of slope is foundational because teaching and learning of slope begins with the question of what slope is.

Research studies define slope in similar ways. Common definitions of slope include geometric ratio, algebraic ratio, physical property, functional property, parametric coefficient, trigonometric conception, calculus conception, and real-world representations (Moore-Russo et al. 2011; Stump 1999). While comprehensive, these definitions can potentially pose difficulties for the purpose of teaching and learning because not only is the list long, but it is not clear from existing literature how these different categories are related to one another (i.e., mathematical coherence), for what purposes (i.e., purposefulness), and under what context to use which definition (i.e., connectedness).

State standards and textbooks (e.g., Burger et al. 2007; Collins et al. 1998; Larson et al. 2004a, b), on the other hand, tend to define slope in terms of the ratio, in particular, what is considered as geometric ratio in terms of "*rise over run*" (Stanton and Moore-Russo 2012). For instance, pre-Common Core California Standards are no exception, except they add the flavor of what is called algebraic ratio, namely, "the vertical change (change in y-value) per unit of horizontal change (change in x-value) is always the same and know that the ratio (rise over run) is called the slope of a graph" (GR7 AF[1]—grade 7: algebra and function strand).

The example definition given above is problematic for several reasons. To begin with, the focus on "rise over run" orients learners' attention on the algorithm for calculation instead of conceptual understanding of what slope is. Secondly, the definition conflates the slope calculated using two points on the line with the slope of the line. In other words, if we were to take two different points, how do we know the ratio will be the same? Further, are we confident that two pairs of points (i.e., four points) are enough to say that any two points will give the same ratio since there are an infinite numbers of points on the line? Finally, the definition assumes teachers and students will know *why* the ratio (of vertical change per unit of horizontal change) is always the same without being given an explanation. These problems make it difficult for the intended users (i.e., teachers and students) to make sense of what slope is. The likely consequence of over-relying on the formulaic definition of slope is that learners will know the formula without understanding what the formula means or why it works. As Walter and Gerson (2007) observed:

> In virtually every classroom in the U.S., students are taught the phrase 'rise over run' as a mnemonic for the algorithm for calculating slope 'change in y, over the change in x,' for an arbitrary pair of points in a coordinate plane. The result of this instrumental device is an instrumental understanding (Skemp 1976/[2006]) of slope as a fraction, with the change in y as the numerator and the change in x as the denominator. Students with this understanding are poorly equipped to make the cognitive leap which seems necessary in order to move from local calculation-based understanding to global understanding of the quotient's meaning for the way a line is positioned in the plane or to make connections with the idea of rate of change. (p. 204)

Consistent with Walter and Gerson's observations, studies have shown that students have difficulties identifying the slope of a line from its graph (Postelnicu and Greenes 2012), computing the slope of a line, or relating slope to the measure of steepness (Postelnicu 2011; Postelnicu and Greenes 2012; Stump 2001b). These difficulties point to the importance of helping students understand why taking any two points on the line will give the same answer and how the slope being the same along the graph controls its shape. The implication is that in order to have a firm understanding of slope, one must understand explicitly the connection between a linear equation and its graph. Indeed, the concept of slope brings forth the need to connect the algebraic aspect of linear equations and the geometric aspect of their graphs.

CCMS Approach to Slope

To remedy how slope has been treated in existing literature, state standards, and textbooks, CCMS presents a coherent learning progression on the topic. According to CCMS, 8th graders are introduced first to an intuitive approach to the concepts of congruence and similarity in order to get comfortable with the angle-angle criterion for similar triangles. Once this groundwork is done, CCMS require that students "use similar triangles to explain why the slope m is the same between any two distinct points on a non-vertical line in the coordinate plane.". By laying a careful foundation of similarity, CCMS not only helps students to make sense of the concept of slope, but also paves the way for students' learning of high-school geometry. A strong foundation in slope also helps students to learn other advanced mathematics topics involving slope, such as functions, down the road. This effort at grade-to-grade continuity and coherence distinguishes CCMS from old practices (Wu 2010b, 2014, 2016a, b).

CCMS emphasizes mathematical reasoning and understanding as the primary focus for students' mathematical learning. To accomplish this learning goal, CCMS carefully sequences mathematical topics so that mathematical concepts learned previously can be used to define, justify and/or prove concepts/ideas students encounter later. Take the concept of slope as an example. Slope features prominently in the teaching of linear equations in the K-12 curriculum. As pointed out previously, much of the emphasis in pre-CCMS curriculum and textbooks focuses more on the mechanics of the calculation rather than on the conceptual understanding of the concept of slope or the connection between a linear equation and its graph. Therefore, students typically learn slope by rote and are not provided with the reasoning why slope is the same regardless of which two distinct points on the line are used to calculate the slope (Walter and Gerson 2007; Wu 2014).

In contrast, CCMS provides 8th graders with an intuitive approach to congruence and similarity by getting them comfortable with the angle-angle criterion for similar triangles. Following this, CCMS requires that 8th graders use similar triangles to explain why the slope of a non-vertical line can be calculated using any two distinct points on the line. Teaching similarity to help students make sense of the concept of slope equips them with a powerful tool to solve all sorts of linear equation problems without having to resort to memorizing different forms of linear equations (i.e., two-point, point-slope, slope-intercept, and standard forms), because now students are provided with the explicit knowledge and understanding that slope can be calculated using any two points on the line that suit one's purpose (for examples, see Newton and Poon 2015a, b).

Furthermore, CCMS' approach to slope connects the algebra of the linear equation and the geometry of the slope. This interconnectedness helps students see how slope being the same all along the graph controls its shape (Wu 2016a, b). Finally, understanding similarity helps students to build a foundation for learning high-school geometry. A solid understanding of slope is foundational for studying other advanced topics involving slope such as functions. CCMS's effort at maintaining grade-to-grade mathematical continuity represents a significant departure from the old curriculum that is characterized as "a mile wide but an inch deep" (Schmidt et al. 2001). The rationale for CCMS' effort at promoting and emphasizing content understanding is best captured by the following paragraph:

> Students who lack understanding of a topic may rely on procedures too heavily. Without a flexible base from which to work, they may be less likely to consider analogous problems, represent problems coherently, justify conclusions, apply the mathematics to practical situations, use technology mindfully to work with the mathematics, explain the mathematics accurately to other students, step back for an overview, or deviate from a known procedure to find a shortcut. In short, a lack of understanding effectively prevents a student from engaging in the mathematical practices. (CCMS)

Response to the Slope Question: A Sample Response Exhibiting Deep Understanding

A response representing deep understanding of slope begins with the definition of the slope of a line:

> *The key mathematical idea underlying this question is that the slope of a line can be calculated using any two points on the line (i.e., independent of any two distinct points on the line). So how can we help students learn this key idea? Before I use P_1, P_2, P_3, P_4 as shown in the picture, I would first review with students how the slope of a line is defined: given a line and assuming it slants upward (as the picture shows), let's take a point P on the line, go 1 unit horizontally to point R, then go upward (or vertically) and let the vertical line from R intersect the given line at point Q. Then the definition of slope is the length of segment QR (i.e., |QR|).*

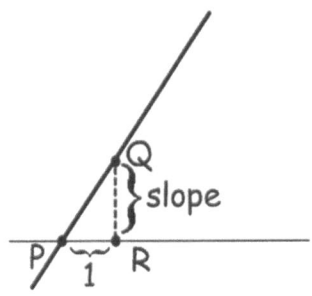

Here the respondent is laying a foundation for what comes next by precisely defining the slope of a line and showing this on the graph. Note how the respondent expands the definition and stretches students' thinking by posing the next question:

> *But how are we certain that this vertical length $|QR|$ is the same for any point P we choose on the line? In other words: if we take another point P' on the line, go 1 unit horizontally to point R' and then go upward to intersect the line at point Q', how do we know that $|QR| = |Q'R'|$?*

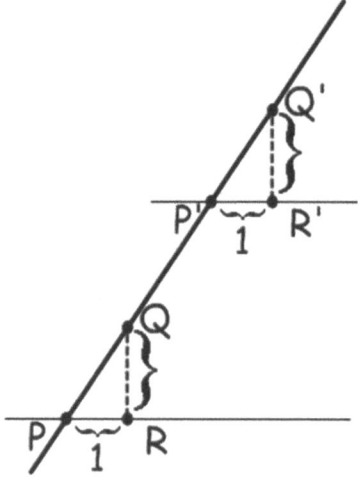

To answer this question, students need to invoke their knowledge of similar triangles. This is an important step towards defining the slope precisely and completely, as the respondent points out:

> *I would expect the following explanation from students: $|\angle PQR| = |\angle P'Q'R'|$, $|\angle QPR| = |\angle Q'P'R'|$ (corresponding angles on parallel lines) and $|PR| = |P'R'|$ = 1, so by the angle-angle-side criterion, $\triangle PQR \cong \triangle P'Q'R'$ and, thus, $|QR| = |Q'R'|$. Therefore, the slope is independent of the point P and it makes sense to talk about the slope of the line.*

With the definition complete, the respondent adds complexity by posing the following question: *"Can we find another, more flexible way of finding the slope of a line, without having to measure 1 unit horizontally from a point on the line and then the vertical distance up?"* This step builds on the previous step of defining the slope of the line but uses similar ideas (i.e., similar triangle), as shown below:

> *To answer this question, let's do the following: let P, Q, R be as before (i.e., P is any point on the line used to define the slope of the line) and now suppose we take any other point on the line, call it S. From S, draw a vertical line and let it meet the horizontal line PR at point T.*

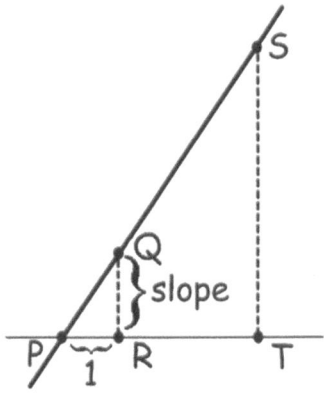

> So now look at the two triangles, $\triangle PQR$ and $\triangle PST$. What can we say about them? Hopefully students would recognize that they are similar triangles; if not, I'd tell them but ask them to prove (explain) why the triangles are similar (by the angle-angle criterion: right angles formed by perpendicular lines and corresponding angles on parallel lines).
>
> After establishing the fact that $\triangle PQR \sim \triangle PST$, I would then ask: what can we say about the relationship between the sides of the triangles? One of the things I would expect students to mention would be:

$$\frac{|QR|}{|ST|} = \frac{|PR|}{|PT|}$$

Then I would guide them to manipulate the above equation into the following:

$$\frac{|QR|}{|ST|} = \frac{|PR|}{|PT|} \Rightarrow |QR| = \frac{|PR| \cdot |ST|}{|PT|} \Rightarrow \frac{|QR|}{|PR|} = \frac{|ST|}{|PT|}$$

At this point, I would ask students what they observe. Hopefully they would recognize that, since |PR|=1, the left side of the equation is equal to line segment |QR|, which is the slope of the line. In other words:

$$slope = \frac{|ST|}{|PT|}$$

Of course, the respondent is very purposeful about why they are doing this exercise:

From this exercise, I would hope students reached the following conclusions:

1. *The slope of the line can be calculated using points P (the point we used to define the slope) and S (any other point on the line).*
2. *We can calculate the slope of a line by dividing the length of the vertical line segment by the length of the horizontal line segment of △PST.*

Because we had shown earlier that the point P used to define the slope is arbitrary (i.e., can be any point on the line) and we had defined S to be another arbitrary point on the line, then the conclusions above can be generalized into the following:

1. *The slope of the line can be calculated using any two distinct points, P and S, on the line.*
2. *We can calculate the slope of a line by dividing the length of the vertical line segment by the length of the horizontal line segment of △PST.*

This purposefulness brings mathematical closure to students and we see how the respondent is very deliberate in scaffolding key ideas throughout the process. Having shown the underlying key ideas, the respondent then goes back to the original question (i.e., using P_1, P_2, P_3, and P_4) and has students work out the proof on their own:

To reinforce these main ideas, I would have students work in groups or pairs to prove (using similar triangle properties) that the slope of the line calculated by P_1, P_2 (in the original graph above) is the same as the slope calculated by P_3, P_4. Once they finish working in groups, I'd have a whole-class discussion and ask students to show how they did the proof. Below is an example of what I'd expect:

Draw in the horizontal and vertical lines through points P_1, P_2, P_3, P_4 and let them intersect at points Q and R as shown below:

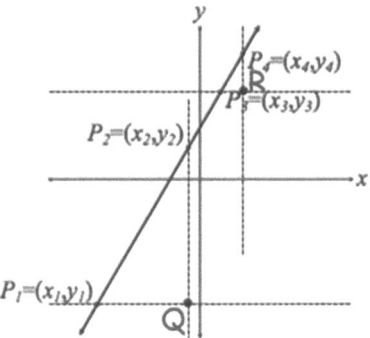

We claim that the two triangles formed, ΔP_1P_2Q and ΔP_3P_4R, are similar. The reason is: $|\angle P_1QP_2|=|\angle P_3RP_4|$ because both equal 90° and $|\angle P_1P_2Q|=|\angle P_3P_4R|$ because they are corresponding angles on parallel lines. Then, by the angle-angle criterion, $\Delta P_1P_2Q \sim \Delta P_3P_4R$. By the key triangle similarity theorem, we can then say $\dfrac{|P_2Q|}{|P_4R|} = \dfrac{|P_1Q|}{|P_3R|}$, and by multiplying both sides of the equation by $|P_4R|$ and $\dfrac{1}{|P_1Q|}$, we get $\dfrac{|P_2Q|}{|P_1Q|} = \dfrac{|P_4R|}{|P_3R|}$. That means the slope calculated by P_1, P_2 is the same as the slope calculated by P_3, P_4. Therefore, the slope can be calculated by any two distinct points on the line. And what is the length of the line segment for P_2 Q and P_1 Q respectively? From the graph, we see that it's $y_2 - y_1$ and $x_2 - x_1$. Similarly, we would get $y_4 - y_3$ and $x_4 - x_3$ for the length of the line segment for P_4 R and P_3 R respectively. What does all this tell us? It means that slope of the line could be represented as the ratio of $\dfrac{y_2 - y_1}{x_2 - x_1}$, or of $\dfrac{y_4 - y_3}{x_4 - x_3}$. This is where the popular phrase "rise over run" came about.

Looking at this response overall, we see that the respondent is mindful of the purpose of each activity, focuses on the key ideas and scaffolds these key ideas in a coherent way, starting with the definition, using it as a basis for subsequent logical reasoning, and leading students from simple ideas to more complex ones, from specific examples to general cases.

To what extent do the sampled students exhibit such understanding? What does their current understanding of slope look like? Content analysis of students' responses reveal several key patterns with regards to their understanding of slope. These patterns and insights derived from them are discussed in the following sections.

Defining Slope Formulaically as Consistent with the K-12 Textbooks (Rise Over Run)

All of the students in the study sample exhibit one qualitative characteristic in their responses which is to define slope formulaically in one way or another, consistent with how slope is defined in the K-12 textbooks (i.e., rise over run) as shown in the following example:

You know that slope = $\frac{rise}{run}$

change in y, tells you the rise

change in x tells you the run

so   slope = $\frac{y_2 - y_1}{x_2 - x_1}$

It doesn't matter what point you choose to subtract from, you just need to make sure x and y correspond to each other. For example, if you subtract y_1 from y_2 then you also need to subtract x_1 from x_2.

Students' responses such as this example show how deeply entrenched students' K-12 learning is. It signals the tendency of these STEM majors to resort to what they have learned as K-12 students to teach the concept as they were taught themselves.

Further examination of some students' responses reveals some ambiguity on their part as to what rise over run really means. For instance, one student said slope is "how much a graph goes in the x-axis and how far a graph goes on the y-axis"; another student stated, "I would explain that the slope is the change between two points. This 'rise' of the 'run' that happens to get from one point to another"; and a third student described, "The slope of a line is just the ratio of the change in the y-values to the change in x values." It is not clear what it means for a graph to go both in the x-axis and y-axis directions. And it is not accurate to say slope moves point A to point B (how and where) or slope is the change in the y-values to the change in x-values (which y's and x's?). The inaccuracy in these responses suggests that students are not making a connection between a linear equation and its graph (i.e., the graph of a linear equation is a collection of all points of ordered pairs (x, y) that satisfy the linear equation). To some extent, this finding is not surprising, since the graph of a linear equation is not defined for them when they first learned the topic as K-12 students. Without connecting a linear equation with its graph, students will not be able to see the connections between: (1) how slope of a line is defined (using their language, how much "rise" from a given one-unit "run" in the Cartesian plane), (2) the formula used to calculate the slope using two distinct points on the line, and (3) why the calculation does not depend on which two distinct points one uses (i.e., they will always give the same answer).

Taking What Needs to Be Proven as Given (i.e., Circular Reasoning)

The scenario asked for the proof that the slope of the line can be calculated using *any* two distinct points on the line. The majority of the responses took what needs to be proven as given as shown in this typical example:

The slope of the line = $\frac{rise}{run}$ = $\frac{\Delta y}{\Delta x}$. Therefore you can take any two points on the graph and find the slope, because the ratio of $\frac{\Delta y}{\Delta x}$ is constant on a straight line. With points P_1 and P_2, you can calculate the slope from $P_1(x_1, y_1)$ $P_2(x_2, y_2)$ = $\frac{y_2 - y_1}{x_2 - x_1}$ = l. The same can be done with points P_3 and P_4. With $P_3(x_3, y_3)$ and $P_4(x_4, y_4)$, slope = $\frac{y_4 - y_3}{x_4 - x_3}$.

The reasoning process goes that since the slope is constant, the formula using the two pairs of points shown to calculate slope will be the same. Slight variation to this sample response is that some students referenced m, as demonstrated in this example:

First we calculate # one of the slope, say P_1 & P_2, and the result of slope is m_1. Then we can find the y-intercept b using P_1 or P_2 (in this case we use P_1) and slope m_1, which is $Y = m_1 x + b$. Then we take another pair of points on the line, say P_3 & P_4, and calculate the slope = m_2. Since these points is on the same line as P_1 & P_2 because the line contain all $P_1 P_2 P_3$ & P_4. So m_1 must be equal to m_2. We can ...

As shown in the above example, the student reasoned that using P_1 and P_2 will give slope m_1 and using P_3 and P_4 will give slope m_2. Since the four points are on the same line, m_1 must be equal to m_2. But what the question is asking for is *why* the slope is the same and *why ANY* two distinctive points will give the same answer.

Some students conflate demonstrating with a few examples with what counts as a mathematical proof, as shown in this example:

$$m = \frac{y_2 - y_1}{x_2 - x_1} = \frac{y_3 - y_1}{x_3 - x_1}$$

- I would give students the slope formula and to test for themselves that any two points work for finding slope.

It is good pedagogical practice to use exploration and draw a tentative hypothesis based on a few examples. But it is not good to equate demonstrating with a few examples with what proof means. How do we know that all points beyond the few examples will work in the same way? This is the focus question that we expect K-12 students to be able to show through proof. Consequently, we expect future mathematics teachers to be able to do the proof themselves as well.

When Similar Triangle Is Mentioned, How Was It Used and for What Purpose?

A few students mentioned similar triangle in their responses but were vague about why the concept of similar triangle is relevant in this context. For instance, one student mentioned that, "first I would make sure students understand the concept of similarity of triangles and then from this non-vertical line, construct a relationship of slopes and triangles, and that the idea of slopes is basically an idea that follows from similar triangles and the ratios of their hypotenuses.". It was not clear what this student meant by "constructing a relationship of slopes and triangles." On the other hand, the term "slopes" suggests there is more than one slope (of the non-vertical line). Also it is incorrect to say that, "slopes...are ratios of their hypotenuses." Examples like this call into question whether students really know why the similar triangle concept is the key to understanding the independence of points when calculating the slope of a line using two distinct points on the line. Furthermore, the responses showed inaccuracy (ratio of their hypotenuses).

A few students explained why similar triangles are relevant, but even these students relied on slope = m = rise over run, showing on the graph which line segment is rise and which is run, and then jumping directly to rise/run (line segment) is the same due to similar triangles, as demonstrated by this example.

There were some inaccuracies here because similar triangles only tell us $|P_4B|/|P_2A| = |P_3B|/|P_1A|$. Interim steps are needed in order to go from $|P_4B|/|P_2A| = |P_3B|/|P_1A|$ to $|P_4B|/|P_3B| = |P_2A|/|P_1A|$ (which happens to be the slope or "rise/run" as the student wrote). It seems the student knew what the final answer would be but did not show the process of how one could get to it.

In addition to inaccurately articulating the ratios of which pairs of lines were equivalent to each other, other inaccuracies included locating the position of a point incorrectly in the Cartesian plane using the two coordinates (i.e., x-coordinate and y-coordinate) or calculating the length of a segment of a line using the coordinates. In the following example, parallel and perpendicular lines from the points given (i.e., P_1, P_2, P_3, and P_4) were drawn to form two right-angle triangles; however, the points at which the lines intersect were wrongly defined.

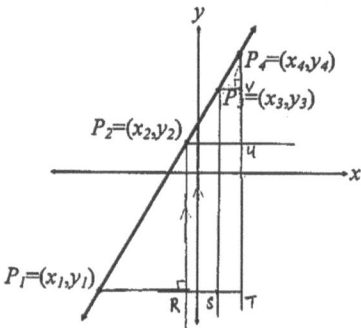

In the above graph, the position of points V and R defined by x and y coordinates should be $V(X_4, Y_3)$ and $R(X_2, Y_1)$ respectively, and not $V(X_3, Y_4)$ and $R(X_1, Y_2)$ as the student stated. And the length of the line segment $|P_1R|$ should be $|X_1| - |X_2|$ and not $X_2 - X_1$ straight out, according to this student (a few others did the same). It seems students who did this were trying to get at the slope formula ($m = Y_2 - Y_1/X_2 - X_1$). But the reasoning for why $|X_1| - |X_2|$ is equivalent to $X_2 - X_1$ is missing. This calls into question whether students really understood the connection between a linear equation and its graph and other mathematical concepts such as absolute values.

Variation in Students' Responses

Students' responses were holistically assessed using rubrics outlined in Table 4.1.

Though none of the students in the study sample scored 4's and only about half a dozen students scored 3's, there is distinctive variation in the quality of their understanding. Specifically, those who scored 3's all referenced similar triangles whereas none of the 1's and 2's did. Furthermore, all but one of these study participants (i.e., those scoring 3's) showed the reasoning process of why similar triangles are important in understanding the independence of points used to calculate

Table 4.1 Rubrics for scoring mathematical content understanding

Levels	Descriptions	Distribution (%)
1: little understanding	Responses completely lack precision, coherence, and purposefulness. For instance, responses are too vague, irrelevant, incomplete, fragmented, inaccurate, or incorrect.	65
2: instrumental understanding	Responses do not meet the criteria of precision, coherence, and purposefulness. However, responses address the questions and have minimal mathematical errors. Mathematical understanding tends to focus knowledge at the surface, or mechanical level.	12
3: transitional understanding	Responses show some elements of precision, coherence, and purposefulness. For instance, there is evidence of an attempt or effort to emphasize the key mathematical idea, its rationale, the logical progression of mathematical concepts, and the connectedness among different mathematical concepts, procedures, and ideas. In addition, responses show an attempt to scaffold mathematical ideas for students.	23
4: relational understanding	Responses exemplify precision, coherence, and purposefulness. There is consistent (or substantial) evidence of an attempt or effort to emphasize the key mathematical idea, its rationale, the logical progression of mathematical concepts, and the connectedness among different mathematical concepts, procedures, and ideas. In addition, responses show attention as to how to scaffold mathematical ideas to students (e.g., from simple to complex; from specific to general).	0

slope. In contrast, those scoring 1's and 2's mostly invoked the formula of slope calculation and engaged in circular reasoning. In general, attempts to emphasize the key mathematical idea, its rationale, the logical progression of mathematical concepts, and the connectedness among different mathematical concepts, procedures, and ideas are fairly consistent among the highest scoring respondents (i.e., those scored 3's) but notably absent among the lowest scoring respondents (those scored 1's). In addition, attention to scaffolding ideas in a systematic and coherent way is present in some responses that scored 3's but missing in responses that scored 1's or 2's. Interestingly, participants who scored 3's were the ones who had taken the mathematics course sequence that deals with mathematical topics at secondary level.

[Note: Even among those who scored 3's, there was a lack of inaccuracy here and there. For instance, mis-identification of which ratios of pairs of legs were equivalent to each other in similar right-angled triangles is common. In addition, all of them defined slope formulaically.]

What Do We Observe Comparing Students' Responses to the Response Exhibiting Deep Understanding?

Several key differences emerge when we compare these STEM majors' responses to the response exhibiting deep understanding of slope. First, all respondents define slope formulaically as rise over run using two points on the line (or symbolically as $\frac{y_2 - y_1}{x_2 - x_1}$). Defining slope in this way in our view creates several conceptual difficulties for learners. To begin with, how do we know any two points will work? Secondly, what does it really mean slope is change in y with unit change in x (where in the formula did unit come into play)? Thirdly, what is the connection between the algebraic expression of slope and its graphical/geometric representation? In contrast, the level 4 response defines the slope by directly using the graph of the linear equation and shows on the graph what it means slope is the rise of y over 1 unit of x *and* that this definition of slope is independent of the point chosen. Once the definition of slope is complete, the response builds on the definition and scaffolds students through a purposeful and coherent process to derive the key ideas that slope of a line can be calculated using any two distinct points, for example P and S, on the line and that we can calculate the slope of a line by dividing the length of the vertical line segment by the length of the horizontal line segment of ΔPST (see Fig. 4.1). This purposefulness brings mathematical closure to students.

Second, a majority of respondents took what needs to be proven as given and engaged in circular reasoning. In other words, instead of proving

Fig. 4.1 Calculating slope of a line

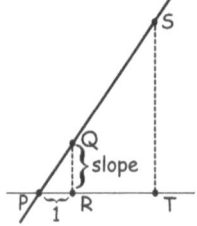

that the slope of a line can be calculated using any two distinct points on the line, they started with the premise that the slope is constant and therefore the formula definition of slope using the two pairs of points shown on the graph is the same. A few considered using a good pedagogical practice of exploration (i.e., try a few points and observe); however, they conflated demonstration through a few examples with mathematical proof. In other words, as there are an infinite number of points on a line, how do we know, beyond the sampled points, that the rest will work the same way as the sampled ones?

Finally, students' responses reveal inaccuracies in terms of articulating the ratios of which pairs of lines were equivalent to each other in similar triangles, locating the position of a point correctly in the Cartesian plane using the two coordinates (i.e., x-coordinate and y-coordinate), or calculating the length of a segment of the horizontal (or vertical) line using the coordinates. These inaccuracies make one wonder if the difficulties were caused by not having the opportunity to learn the connection between a linear equation and its graph or by a lack of understanding of what the meaning of a line is (i.e., the definition of a line).

These weaknesses in responses show gaps in these STEM majors' conceptual understanding of slope and of the connection between a linear equation and its graph. These students were STEM majors at one of the elite research universities. They represent some of the strongest pool of candidates for future mathematics teachers in terms of subject matter knowledge. Even these students struggled with proving that the slope of a line can be calculated by using *any* two distinct points on the line. It is important to emphasize that the intention is not to criticize their lack of conceptual understanding of slope. Rather the results signal how important it is to lay a strong foundation of mathematics topics at K-12 level, because that is where future mathematics teachers learn topics that they will one day teach (given the current mathematics education system).

IMPLICATIONS FOR MATHEMATICS TEACHERS' CONTENT TRAINING AT THE COLLEGE LEVEL

Data in this chapter show that the STEM majors in the study sample do not possess a deep understanding of the slope concept. Even though these STEM majors might be strong in their disciplinary knowledge, they do not necessarily have the depth of understanding of slope in order to teach at the level that is required by the new CCMS.

Furthermore, the small number of participants who scored 3's are mathematics majors who were taking Mathematics of the Secondary School Curriculum, a three-semester course sequence designed to teach grades 6–12 content to mathematics majors interested in pursuing teaching as a career. The principles underlying this course sequence reflect and are consistent with CCMS's emphasis on reasoning and conceptual understanding. Non-mathematics majors or mathematics majors who were not taking Mathematics of the Secondary School Curriculum mostly scored 1's or 1's and 2's, and none scored 3's. These results signal the importance of explicitly teaching future mathematics teachers the content knowledge that they will be teaching to their students down the road.

As mentioned in the finding section, the characteristics of study participants' understanding of the slope concept revealed gaps in their conceptual understanding of slope and of the connection between a linear equation and its graph. These students were STEM majors at one of the top research universities. Even these students struggled with proving that the slope of a line can be calculated by using *any* two distinctive points on the line.

Taken together, these findings have important implications for the content training of future mathematics teachers in the era of CCMS in order to increase the quality of the teaching force in terms of their content preparation. The focus on STEM majors is significant, because they represent the strongest pool of future mathematics teachers. In both research and practice, a college major in mathematics is used to signal a candidate's content knowledge for teaching K-12 students, assuming that mathematics majors have the deep understanding of the K-12 topics to teach well at that level. This assumption is manifested to some extent in the recent efforts at recruiting undergraduate STEM majors into teaching through programs such as 100 k10 in New York, UTeach in Texas, and UTeach replication sites across the country.

What has not been brought to the forefront is the fact that the content focus of typical college mathematics courses serves a different purpose from content needed for teaching at the K-12 level (Askey 1999; Wu 2010a, 2011a). Consequently, the most direct resource for mathematics teachers, whether mathematics majors or not, to learn what they are supposed to teach is the mathematics they learned as K-12 students, as shown in our study of their understanding of slope. Interestingly, one of the strongest oppositions to states adopting CCMS is the push against the federal government shoveling down a set of national standards onto local states. What these opponents failed to realize is the fact that there has been a de facto national mathematics curriculum at work, which is regarded as text-book school mathematics (TSM) (Wu 2011c, d, 2014, 2015). TSM lacks the mathematical rigor, focus, and coherence that CCMS calls for. It is therefore reasonable to assume that students who went through TSM will not be adequately prepared to teach mathematics at the level that CCMS calls for, as supported by the findings of this study.

Data reported in this chapter are set within a broader investigation of STEM majors' mathematical content understanding of three critical early algebra topics (Newton and Poon 2015a). The findings on students' understanding of slope mirror those from the broader study, which brings us to the general issue of mathematics teachers' content training.

Subject matter knowledge plays a central role in teaching (Ball et al. 2005, 2008; Baumert et al. 2010; Buchmann 1984; Ma 1999, 2010; Shulman 1986). In both research and practice, a college major in mathematics is used to signal a candidate's content knowledge for teaching K-12 students, assuming that mathematics majors have the deep understanding of the K-12 topics to teach well at that level. What has not been brought to the forefront is the fact that the content focus of typical college mathematics courses serves a different purpose from content needed for teaching at the K-12 level (Askey 1999; Ball 1990; Wu 2011a). Though efforts at recruiting undergraduate STEM majors to improve the quality of the teaching force in mathematics are commendable, we need to provide recruits with explicit content training of mathematics topics that they are expected to teach at the K-12 level. Otherwise, STEM majors will resort to the way they were taught as K-12 students when they become teachers, as signaled by the data in this chapter.

Because college mathematics (i.e., the content most teachers learned before becoming teachers) has little use in the K-12 classroom (Wu 2011a, b), K-12 mathematics textbooks become the primary source of subject matter knowledge for teachers. The problems with K-12 textbooks have been well documented by mathematicians and Wu labels such knowledge rooted in K-12 textbooks as TSM (Wu 2011a, d).

TSM is problematic because it goes against the five fundamental principles of mathematics (FPM) outlined by Wu (2011e), a mathematician who has devoted more than a decade of effort at addressing K-12 mathematics teachers' content knowledge. The five FPM are:

1. Every concept has a precise definition, and definitions furnish the basis for logical reasoning. (Definitions leave no doubt about what exactly students have to learn.)
2. Mathematical statements are precise. Precision makes possible the distinction between what is known and what is not known, and what is true and what is false. (Precision eliminates the need to guess in learning mathematics.)
3. Every assertion is supported by logical reasoning. There are no arbitrary or irrational decrees in mathematics. (Mathematics is learnable because it is reasonable.)
4. Mathematics is coherent. Mathematics is a living organism in which all the different parts are interconnected. (Mathematics is not a bag of isolated tricks for students to memorize.)
5. Mathematics is purposeful. Every concept and skill in the school mathematics curriculum is there for a purpose. (Students get to know where they are headed.)

To remedy the inadequate content preparation of mathematics teachers, data in this chapter suggest that teachers will need opportunities to be engaged in explicit, systematic, and rigorous content training of topics that they are charged to teach. These opportunities can come from preservice, specially designed, mathematics courses. For example, the UC Berkeley's Department of Mathematics is one of the few that offer courses specifically focusing on grades 6–12 content for mathematics majors who are interested in pursuing teaching as a career. We need policies that promote college mathematics departments' involvement in the training of future mathematics teachers (Shulman 1999).

Findings presented in this chapter also have implications for using teachers' college mathematics coursework as a proxy measure of their content knowledge as many empirical studies have done. Empirical studies on the relationship between teachers' college mathematics coursework and their students' mathematical performance have yielded mixed results. One possible explanation might be that having advanced mathematical knowledge at college level does not necessarily equate with having a deep understanding of K-12 content, which is necessary in order to translate this deep understanding into effective classroom practices in terms of engaging K-12 students around substantive mathematics. Therefore, instead of using proxy measures such as college mathematics coursework, directly measuring teachers' understanding of K-12 content they teach may help to produce consistent results on the relationship between teachers' mathematical knowledge and students' achievement.

Finally, the study findings could have potential implications for the professional development of in-service teachers in order to teach CCMS. Since most teachers did not have the opportunities to learn the content knowledge they need to teach from their college mathematics courses, they typically resort to the way they were taught as K-12 students (Adams and Krockover 1997; Lortie 1975). To improve the quality of teachers' content understanding according to CCMS, we need in-service professional development activities that focus explicitly on the content knowledge they are teaching and at the level of rigor that is required by CCMS. But opportunities for teachers to continue to grow their understanding of mathematics they teach are rather limited. This topic is discussed in Chap. 5.

NOTE

1. GR7 AF stands for Grade 7 Algebra and Function.

REFERENCES

Adams, P. E., & Krockover, G. H. (1997). Beginning science teacher cognition and its origins in the pre-service secondary science teacher program. *Journal of Research in Science Teaching, 34*(6), 633–653.

Askey, R. (1999). Knowing and teaching elementary mathematics. *American Educator, 23*, 1–8.

Ball, D. L. (1990). The mathematical understanding that prospective teachers bring to teacher education. *Elementary School Journal, 90*, 449–466.

Ball, D. L., Hill, H. C., & Bass, H. (2005). Knowing mathematics for teaching: Who knows mathematics well enough to teach third grade, and how can we decide? *American Educator, 29*(3), 14.

Ball, D. L., Hoover, M. H., & Phelps, G. (2008). Content knowledge for teaching: What makes it special. *Journal of Teacher Education, 59*(5), 389–407.

Barr, G. (1980). Graphs, gradients, and intercepts. *Mathematics in School, 9*(1), 5–6.

Barr, G. (1981). Some student ideas on the concept of gradient. *Mathematics in School, 10*(1), 14–17.

Baumert, J., Kunter, M., Blum, W., Brunner, M., Voss, T., Jordan, A., & Klusmann, U. (2010). Teachers' mathematical knowledge, cognitive activation in the classroom, and student progress. *American Educational Research Journal,* *47*(1), 133–180.

Buchmann, M. (1984). The priority of knowledge and understanding in teaching. In J. Raths & L. Katz (Eds.), *Advances in teacher education* (Vol. 1, pp. 29–48). Norwood: Ablex.

Burger, E. B., Chard, D. J., Hall, E. J., Kennedy, P. A., Leinwand, S. J., Renfro, F. L., & Waits, B. K. (2007). *Algebra 1.* Orlando: Holt, Rinehart and Winston.

Collins, W., Foster, A. G., Winters, L. J., Swart, W. L., Cuevas, G. J., Rath, J., & Gordon, B. (1998). *Algebra 1: Integration applications connections.* New York: Glencoe/McGraw-Hill.

Greenes, C., Chang, K. Y., & Ben-Chaim, D. (2007). *International survey of high school students' understanding of key concepts of linearity.* Proceedings of the 31st conference of the international group for the psychology of mathematics education (Vol. 2, pp. 273–280). Seoul. Retrieved August 18, 2013, from http://eric.ed.gov/PDFS/ED499417.pdf

Hauger, G. S. (1997). *Growth of knowledge of rate in four precalculus students.* Paper presented at the annual meeting of the American Educational Research Association, Chicago.

Larson, R., Boswell, L., Kanold, T. D., & Stiff, L. (2004a). *Algebra 1.* Evanston: McDougal Littell.

Larson, R., Boswell, L., Kanold, T. D., & Stiff, L. (2004b). *Algebra 1: Concepts and skills.* Evanston: McDougal Littell.

Leinhardt, G., Zaslavsky, O., & Stein, M. K. (1990). Functions, graphs, and graphing: Tasks, learning, and teaching. *Review of Educational Research, 60,* 1–64.

Lobato, J. (1996). *Transfer reconceived: How "sameness" is produced in mathematics activity.* Doctoral dissertation. Retrieved from ProQuest Dissertations and Theses.

Lobato, J. (2008). When students don't apply the knowledge you think they have, rethink your assumptions about transfer. In M. P. Carlson & C. Rasmussen (Eds.), *Making the connection: Research and teaching in undergraduate mathematics education* (pp. 289–304). Washington, DC: Mathematical Association of America.

Lobato, J., & Siebert, D. (2002). Quantitative reasoning in a reconceived view of transfer. *Journal of Mathematical Behavior, 21,* 87–116.

Lobato, J., & Thanheiser, E. (1999). Re-thinking slope from quantitative and phenomenological perspectives. In F. Hitt & M. Santos (Eds.), *Proceedings of the 21st annual meeting of the North American chapter of the international group for the psychology of mathematics education* (Vol. 1, pp. 291–297). Columbus: ERIC. (ERIC Document Reproduction Service No. ED 433998).

Lobato, J., & Thanheiser, E. (2002). Developing understanding of ratio-as-measure as a foundation for slope. In B. Litwiller (Ed.), *Making sense of fractions, ratios, and proportions: 2002 yearbook* (pp. 162–175). Reston: National Council of Teachers of Mathematics.

Lortie, D. (1975). *Schoolteacher: A sociological study.* Chicago: University of Chicago Press.

Ma, L. (1999). *Knowing and teaching elementary mathematics: Teachers' understanding of fundamental mathematics in China and the United States.* Mahwah: Lawrence Erlbaum Associates.

Ma, L. (2010). *Knowing and teaching elementary mathematics: Teachers' understanding of fundamental mathematics in China and the United States* (2nd ed.). New York: Routledge.

Moore-Russo, D., Conner, A., & Rugg, K. I. (2011). Can slope be negative in 3-space? Studying concept image of slope through collective definition construction. *Educational Studies in Mathematics, 76*(1), 3–21.

Newton, X., & Poon, R. (2015a). Mathematical content understanding for teaching: A study of undergraduate STEM majors. *Creative Education, 6*(10), 998–1031. https://doi.org/10.4236/ce.2015.610101.

Newton, X., & Poon, R. (2015b). Pre-service STEM majors' understanding of slope according to common core mathematics standards: An exploratory study. *Global Journal of Human Social Science Research, 15*(7), 27–42.

Postelnicu, V. (2011). *Student difficulties with linearity and linear functions and teachers' understanding of student difficulties.* Doctoral dissertation. Retrieved from ProQuest Dissertations and Theses.

Postelnicu, V., & Greenes, C. (2012). Do teachers know what their students know? National council of supervisors of mathematics. *Newsletter, 42*(3), 14–15.

Schmidt, W. H., & Houang, R. (2012). Curricular coherence and the common core state standards for mathematics. *Educational Researcher, 41*(8), 294–308.

Schmidt, W. H., McKnight, C. C., Houang, R. T., Wang, H., Wiley, D. E., Cogan, L. S., & Wolfe, R. G. (2001). *Why schools matter: A cross-national comparison of curriculum and learning.* San Francisco: Jossey-Bass.

Schmidt, W. H., Houang, R., & Cogan, L. S. (2011). Preparing future math teachers. *Science, 332,* 1266–1267. Education Forum.

Shulman, L. S. (1986). Those who understand: Knowledge growth in teaching. *Educational Researcher, 15*(2), 4–14.

Shulman, L. S. (1999). Forward. In L. Ma (Ed.), *Knowing and teaching elementary mathematics: Teachers' understanding of fundamental mathematics in China and the United States.* Mahwah: Lawrence Erlbaum Associates, Inc.

Skemp, R. R. (1976/2006). Relational understanding and instrumental understanding. *Mathematics Teaching in the Middle School, 12*(2), 88–95. Originally published in *Mathematics Teaching.*

Stanton, M., & Moore-Russo, D. (2012). Conceptualizations of slope: A review of state standards. *School Science and Mathematics, 112*(5), 270–277.

Stump, S. L. (1996). *Secondary mathematics teachers' knowledge of the concept of slope.* Doctoral dissertation. Retrieved from ProQuest Dissertations and Theses.

Stump, S. L. (1997, March). *Secondary mathematics teachers' knowledge of the concept of slope*. Paper presented at the annual meeting of the American Educational Research Association, Chicago.

Stump, S. L. (1999). Secondary mathematics teachers' knowledge of slope. *Mathematics Education Research Journal, 11*(2), 124–144.

Stump, S. L. (2001a). Developing preservice teachers' pedagogical content knowledge of slope. *Journal of Mathematical Behavior, 20*, 207–227.

Stump, S. L. (2001b). High school precalculus students' understanding of slope as measure. *School Science and Mathematics, 101*(2), 81–89.

Teuscher, D., & Reys, R. E. (2010). Slope, rate of change, and steepness: Do students understand these concepts? *Mathematics Teacher, 103*(7), 519–524.

Walter, J. G., & Gerson, H. (2007). Teachers' personal agency: Making sense of slope through additive structures. *Educational Studies in Mathematics, 65*(2), 205–233.

Wu, H. S. (2010a). *The mathematics teachers should know*. Talk given at Lisbon, Portugal, on January 29, 2010. Accessible at: http://math.berkeley.edu/~wu/Lisbon2010_2.pdf

Wu, H. S. (2010b). *Introduction to school algebra*. Accessible at: http://math.berkeley.edu/~wu/Algebrasummary.pdf

Wu, H. S. (2011a). The miss-education of mathematics teachers. *Notices of the American Mathematical Society, 58*(3), 372–384.

Wu, H. S. (2011b). *Understanding numbers in elementary school mathematics*. Providence: American Mathematical Society.

Wu, H. S. (2011c). *Professional development and textbook school mathematics*. Accessible at: http://math.berkeley.edu/~wu/AMS COE 2011.pdf

Wu, H. S. (2011d). Phoenix rising. Bringing the common core state mathematics standards to life. *American Educator, 35*(3), 3–13. Accessible at: http://www.aft.org/pdfs/americaneducator/fall2011/Wu.pdf.

Wu, H. S. (2011e). *The mathematics early grade teachers need to know| and what it means to know it*. Talk given at Rio de Janeiro. Accessible at: https://math.berkeley.edu/~wu/Brazil2.pdf

Wu, H. S. (2014). Potential impact of the common core mathematics standards on the American curriculum. In Y. Li & G. Lappan (Eds.), *Mathematics curriculum in school education: Advances in mathematics education* (pp. 119–142). Dordrecht: Springer.

Wu, H. S. (2015). *Textbook school mathematics and the preparation of mathematics teachers*. Accessible at: https://math.berkeley.edu/~wu/Stony_Brook_2014.pdf

Wu, H. S. (2016a). *Teaching school mathematics: Pre-algebra*. Providence: American Mathematical Society.

Wu, H. S. (2016b). *Teaching school mathematics: Algebra*. Providence: American Mathematical Society.

Zaslavsky, O., Sela, H., & Leron, U. (2002). Being sloppy about slope: The effect of changing the scale. *Educational Studies in Mathematics, 49*(1), 119–140.

CHAPTER 5

Opportunities for Teachers to Learn Mathematics Through Professional Development and Instructional Tools

As pointed out in Chap. 3, one of the key factors explaining Chinese students' mathematical performance is that teachers in China continue to have opportunities to learn mathematics throughout their careers (Ma 1999, 2010). The investigation into both teachers' and math coaches' understanding of foundational mathematics topics (i.e., two-digit subtraction with regrouping and multi-digit multiplication) highlights why teachers themselves must develop a deep conceptual understanding of mathematics. These opportunities to learn will come mainly through their participation in various in-service professional development activities and instructional tools developed to support classroom mathematics teaching and learning. These opportunities can influence their ability to both develop their understanding of mathematics they teach and to adopt new beliefs and practices.

This chapter examines one district's reform effort at developing teachers by providing them with mathematics coaching and various instructional tools. This provides a window through which to discuss issues of in-service teachers' opportunities to learn mathematics. This chapter is based on the premise that the education and continued development of teachers is key to students' own learning opportunities. No effort to improve students' mathematics understanding can succeed without parallel attention to their teachers' opportunities for learning. Teachers play a central role in determining what is taught and learned in schools, and how it is taught—a role no curriculum by itself can fulfill.

© The Author(s) 2018

X. A. Newton, *Improving Teacher Knowledge in K-12 Schooling*,
https://doi.org/10.1007/978-3-319-71207-9_5

Context for the District Mathematics Reform Initiative

During the heyday of No Child Left Behind (NCLB), one of the largest urban public school districts in the USA launched a district-wide five-year strategic plan, the District Mathematics Plan (DMP), to improve students' mathematical competencies and give all students access to Algebra by grade 8. The plan aligned instruction, professional development, textbooks, and assessment with the mathematics content standards for the state's public schools. Highlights of the plan included:

- Aligning new textbooks for grades K through Algebra with the state content standards.
- Requiring all students to take Algebra (and Algebra 1 by grade 8) and to pass the state High School Exit Exam in order to graduate.
- Hiring mathematics coaches to support classroom teachers in mathematics.
- Offering on-going, school-based professional development opportunities to teachers.

Two years after the initial adoption of the plan, the DMP augmented the initiative by adding two key components to further support teachers. These two additions include creating the Math Instructional Guide (MIG) and implementing quarterly periodic assessments (PAs). The MIG and PA are intricately linked to each other such that reference to one would be impossible without mentioning the other.

Periodic assessments, designed and developed by the Educational Testing Service (ETS) in collaboration with the district's central mathematics team, were one of the key components of the DMP. The purpose of PAs was diagnostic so that teachers knew which students needed reteaching or intervention based on the test results. The assessments were designed to be aligned with the state mathematics content standards and were administered on a quarterly basis in both English and Spanish in grades K through Algebra 1. The test for kindergarten and grade 1 consisted of 20 multiple-choice (MC) items and one constructed response (CR) item. For grades 2–7 and Algebra 1, the test was comprised of 30 MC items and one CR item, except for the quarter 4 assessment for grades 6 through Algebra 1, which consisted of 60 MC items and one CR item.

The focus of the PA administered during a quarter was based on the content standards outlined in MIG for that quarter. For each quarter, the MIG outlined the content standards to be taught and the lesson(s) in the textbooks that teachers should use to teach the standards. The motivation of the MIG was to align instruction with state standards so that mathematics instruction was standards-driven rather than textbook-driven. Therefore, teachers might be using different textbooks, but their focus of instruction would be on the same standards. The sequencing[1] of different content standards, as outlined in the MIG, provided the basis for the design of the PAs. These two components (i.e., the MIG and PA) along with mathematics coaching have become the key elements of the DMP. These three key elements (MIG, mathematics PAs, and mathematics coaching) are the primary focus of this chapter. These three components involve a large investment of resources and money and are directly related to the areas of curriculum, assessment, and professional development (PD) support, which are important aspects that surround and drive teaching and learning. Examining how these components play themselves out as the reform initiative travels down the school system provides a window through which to understand why the USA has been constantly reforming its mathematics education system and yet little impact is evident in students' performance or the substance of classroom mathematics teaching and learning.

QUALITY OF TEACHERS' OPPORTUNITIES TO LEARN MATHEMATICS THROUGH PD

Teacher development is a vast topic; this chapter focuses strategically on a small set of core issues relevant to understanding the quality of teachers' opportunities to learn mathematics once they become classroom teachers. Specifically, the chapter attends to two aspects that are central to the practice of providing professional development for teachers of mathematics. The two aspects are: (1) whether the focus of professional development is on equipping teachers with the mathematical knowledge and skills that will enable them to teach mathematics effectively, and (2) whether the nature of professional development is conducive to developing and sustaining such sophisticated knowledge on an on-going basis.

The reason for the emphasis on developing teachers' mathematical knowledge and skills as the goal of professional development is twofold: (1) for the purpose of improving students' opportunities to learn mathematics, and (2) for the purpose of improving teachers' opportunities to learn mathematics so as to enable them to teach effectively. How teachers know mathematics is central to their capacity to use instructional materials wisely, to assess students' progress, and to make sound judgments about presentation, emphasis, and sequencing of mathematical ideas. Paradoxically, research has consistently revealed that many teachers lack sound mathematical understanding and skill (e.g., the ability to unpack mathematical ideas, explain procedures, choose and use representations, or appraise unfamiliar mathematical claims and solutions).

To some extent, this finding is unsurprising because teachers, like other adults in the USA, are graduates of the system we seek to improve and their opportunities to learn mathematics have been uneven or inadequate (Ball and Rowan 2004; Cohen and Ball 2001; Hill and Ball 2004; Ma 1999, 2010). Equipping teachers with continued opportunities to deepen their own mathematical understanding through professional development opportunities once they enter the workforce, therefore, is of paramount importance both in terms of their own learning and advancement and in terms of improving students' opportunities to learn mathematics.

Apart from an emphasis on providing teachers with opportunities to deepen their own mathematical understanding, the nature of PD also plays a crucial role in determining the PD effectiveness. Nature is defined as the positive components that characterize an effective PD, which include clearly stated goals, on-going learning opportunities, an emphasis on discussion and reflection, and explicit follow-up plans on how teachers can bring the knowledge and skills back to classroom mathematics teaching and learning. In other words, the nature of PD needs to be conducive to teachers' developing and sustaining sophisticated knowledge.

TYPES AND FOCUS OF MATHEMATICS PD LED BY MATHEMATICS COACHES IN SCHOOLS

Mathematics coaches tended to be the primary trainers of mathematics PD across the schools. School site PD typically occurred in one of three settings: (1) entire staff meetings, (2) grade level or departmental meetings, or (3) coach-teacher one-on-one activities. Although grade level and departmental meetings were led by a teacher 60% of the time (usually a department or grade-level chair) and by a mathematics coach only about 40% of the time, entire staff training was almost always led by the coach, and individual (or one-on-one) training was led by a coach without exception.

Though the mathematics coach was the primary trainer of PD, school site PD tended to focus on the issues of the MIG and PAs rather than on instructional coaching that emphasizes teachers' understanding of subject matter and development of pedagogical skills. Fifty percent of mathematics PD was devoted to logistical and administrative details regarding the use of the MIG and PAs. About 10% of mathematics PD was unrelated to the DMP. Although about 40% of the mathematics PD was devoted to instructional coaching (i.e., coach-teacher working together), only 27% consisted of a coach giving a demonstration lesson and only 8% included a coach giving a demonstration lesson using manipulatives. Since instructional coaching and demonstrations with manipulatives are two of the most promising activities whereby teachers could learn instructional strategies and pedagogies, the following sections examine these activities in detail.

How Did Coaches Employ Manipulatives?

The use of manipulatives by coaches tended to be procedural rather than conceptual. In other words, coaches were focused on the steps involved in using a manipulative rather than on the concept that the manipulatives helped to convey. The following is a typical example of a coach using manipulatives:

C^2:	We see a happy face. We start with a happy face. I will give you some shapes, a brown square and a brown triangle. When you go back to your seats we will sort. Say sort.
Ss:	Sort.
C:	Say group of triangles.
Ss:	[repeat].
C:	Say group of squares.
Ss:	[repeat].
C:	We are going to make a pattern. [C puts down square and triangle....]
C:	Say it with me.
C and Ss:	square, triangle, square....

C: Watch me mix, say mix.
Ss: Mix.
      [C mixes up the shapes.]
C: Put the triangle on this side and the square on this side.
      [C demonstrates.]
C: Group the triangles, group the squares.
      [C chooses GH to group the triangles and BH to group the squares.]
C: Correct?
Ss: Thumbs up.
C: Who can make a pattern? [C puts down a square.] Who can do this?
      [GH puts a square next to the square.]
      [C has her put a triangle down].

In this segment of the demonstration lesson, the coach models a procedure, sorting the triangles from the squares and then making a pattern (the pattern being specifically in terms of triangle, square, triangle, square, and so on alternating the two). Students are then called up to perform these same two actions (i.e., grouping triangles with triangles, squares with squares, and then making the pattern). It seems that the purpose is to get students to imitate the same procedure. A student breaks with this imitation when she forms a pattern other than the one modeled. (Notice that the coach says, "Who can make *a* pattern?" not "Who can replicate the pattern I made?" or "Who can make *this* pattern?" Therefore, this student's pattern is perfectly valid.) Rather than engaging the students about this new pattern, the coach quickly imposes the previously modeled pattern. Implicit in the coach's correction is the idea that to "make a pattern" means to make *this particular* pattern. This limits the concept of what a pattern is to the idea of arranging squares and triangles alternately in a row, that is, the idea of being able to place a square, then a triangle, and then a square and so on. Though manipulatives are used here, the focus is still on procedural imitation rather than on conceptualization of patterns.

Similarly, when demonstrating the use of manipulatives to teachers, coaches tend to focus on the procedural aspects (even prescribe what teachers should do) rather than the concept that the manipulatives help to convey. A typical training for teachers regarding the use of manipulatives is as follows:

C: [Takes out a copy of the "incredible equation."] This was successful at Topeka. The chart is presented and done the first day of the month.
[Coach proceeds to explain the chart as follow: what T should do.]

C: The T will ask, what one means. They[3] know it's the date, they know first in line. T should ask, "Tell me something that makes one." A student will say $1 + 0$ is one. T writes it horizontally, then vertically. When a student says take away, $1 - 0 = 1$, the T also incorporates the = sign. As the month goes on, you add the numbers and it goes to the 100th day. Use a stamp on it that says "good thinking" and the birthday person of the month takes it home. They get an idea that there are many different ways beyond just the fact families. They use greater numbers because of it and they can use their 100's charts.

The coach states that the benefit of the activity is for students to "get an idea [that] there are many different ways beyond the fact families. They use greater numbers because of it and they get to use their 100's charts." While using "greater numbers" and "their 100's charts" does not necessarily translate into conceptual understanding, recognizing that relationships between numbers are not bounded by fact families is important. This could potentially lead students to ideas such as mathematics being fluid rather than rigid, or it being about relationships (i.e., between numbers/quantities) rather than facts, memorization, and procedures.

While the end goal that the coach has for the students is conceptual, the means by which the coach trains the teachers is still purely procedural. The coach gives the teachers specific steps and even questions to ask. This is significant because teachers are being trained with the hope that their teaching will lead to a conceptual understanding among their students, which is that their students will "get an idea there are many different ways beyond fact families." The model of teaching that teachers received in their training from their mathematics coaches, however, focuses on procedural doing rather than developing conceptual understanding.

Content Knowledge as Revealed by the Use
of Manipulatives

Coaches' use of manipulatives reveal an underdeveloped pedagogy and content conceptualization. Often manipulatives are employed in a way that does not make explicit what mathematical concepts are conveyed through the use of manipulatives. This disconnect reveals an underdeveloped pedagogy regarding the use of manipulatives. Take the following as an example where a coach is working with a group of teachers:

C: Let's take a look at this problem. We're looking at $2x + 3 = 7$. This can be very confusing to students who are first learning this. So, we're going to separate them. This number two (2) in the equation…let's say it means two groups. If we say this equation in words, it means, how many pieces of chocolate must two groups have, if both groups added together with three extra chocolate pieces equals seven?

T1:   I think doing that problem first with the math pieces is too complicated for students.

T2:   Yeah, I think they might have a hard time following.

C: Okay. Let's try this. $X + 3 = 7$. How about this?

T1:   Okay, we can do that.

C: So, how will we solve this problem with the math pieces?

T3:   Well, we can say, how many pieces of chocolate must you have had before, if your friend gave you three pieces and now you have a total of seven?

C: Okay, how can you rephrase that into something easier to understand?

T4:   If your friend gives you three pieces of candy and now you have a total of seven. How many must you have had before?

C: Okay, that can work. Anyone else?

T2:   Well, I just think as long as you use an example that students can relate to, it'll be okay.

In this example, it is commendable that teachers are concerned about students not being able to relate to what $2x + 3 = 7$ might mean and suggest they start with a simpler problem ($x + 3 = 7$) instead. Close examination of this set of interactions, however, reveals several troubling issues.

First, the purpose of this training is for the coach to show teachers how to use manipulatives to teach students how to solve equations. But the coach is using plastic manipulatives on an overhead. The same training could have taken place using only a chalkboard as the conversation centered on how to translate a symbolic expression into word problems rather than on how the manipulatives might be used to teach the mathematical topic. In addition, both the coach and the teachers seem to be oblivious to the fact that X is not defined at all during this entire conversation about the equation involving X. Finally, the coach attempts to translate the equation, $2x + 3 = 7$ into a word problem as: "This number two (2) in the equation...let's say it means two groups. If we say this equation in words, it means, how many pieces of chocolate must two groups have, if both groups added together with three extra chocolate pieces equals seven?" In this word problem, the important assumption that each of the two groups has the same number of pieces of chocolate is not stated explicitly. In addition, the question should be "how many pieces of chocolate must *each* of the two groups have" instead of "must two groups have". The subtle distinction is important, because how the problem is phrased relates directly to what the symbol "X" stands for. In totality, the word problem should have read: Assuming two groups of children have the same number of pieces of chocolate and let X stand for the pieces of chocolate each group has, what is X if we add 3 more pieces to the total pieces of chocolate the two groups had and now the two groups have a total of 7?

The same mathematical inaccuracy is evident in demonstration lessons that supposedly use manipulatives for more sophisticated mathematical problems. The following example is among the demonstration lessons involving sophisticated use of manipulatives for teaching how to solve equations of a more sophisticated form involving "X."

C: Now everyone should have 3x equals 5 plus 7 (i.e., $3x = 5 + 7$). 5 plus 7 equals 12. So now we have to find the three variables that equal 12. But they all have to have the same value.
        Chalk board: $12 = \_\_ + \_\_ + \_\_\_$.
C: What can I break 12 into to get three parts?
S: It's 4, because 12 into 3 equals 4.
C: Yes. Could you have 7 plus 3 plus 2 equal x? No because all of the numbers have to be the same.

In this example students were using scales to balance their equations as the coach worked through the problem on the board. The coach told students that they must find three variables that equal 12 but that the variables "have to have the same value." The coach's explanation as to why the numbers cannot be 7, 3, and 2 was simply that "all of the numbers have to be the same." There was no discussion of the idea that "x" represents a particular number in the equation, or even why it would be problematic if "x" were to represent 7, 3, or 2. The coach simply stated the rule that "all of the numbers have to be the same."

The coach's earlier statement that "we have to find the three variables that equal 12. But they all have to have the same value" is also ambiguous (i.e., three variables) and contradictory (i.e., three variables that equal 12 and have to have the same value). A clear and precise definition of "x" would have explained why "x" cannot be 7, 3, or 2 at the *same* time. In other words, x should be clearly defined as: Assuming the equation $3x = 5 + 7$ has a unique solution, "x" stands for the unique number (i.e., solution) that satisfies the equation, or makes the equality of the equation true.

Though these details might seem insignificant to a lay person, accumulations of the failure to attend to such details may be *the* reason why we are not building a sound conceptual groundwork for students in their early encounter with mathematics. Students might be able to solve the equation correctly, but they might not discover the purpose of such activity (i.e., solving "x") or know what it means to solve an equation involving "x" and why they need to learn this. What students are denied is the very thinking process which helps to develop them into independent learners. This again reveals an underdeveloped and short-sighted pedagogy largely attributable to a lack of understanding of the underlying mathematical concepts and purposes.

How Were Individual Teachers Trained by Coaches?

Coach debriefings and planning with teachers also revealed an underdeveloped pedagogy that was procedurally focused. Consider these very typical debriefing sessions between a coach and a teacher.

Example 5.1

C: Last week I did a demo on vocabulary. Did you use that?
T: I've been using the vocabulary all the way through.
C: Have you tried card?
T: No.
C: If you write the word on the card, when you do it ahead of time, or introduce the word from left to right when they are a little more focused. Since you are a new teacher, you will get the same grade level next year.
T: I will? Great!
C: You can put the cards up on your cupboard and later on they can read them when they know the sounds.

Example 5.2

C: Patterns can go horizontal and vertical, moving and exploring on the floor.
    Tomorrow we can start with a human pattern. Stick with the same color, so they don't get mixed up. [C hold up a happy face card.] You can join us if you feel comfortable. My follow up is a reinforcement of what we have done. You've done triangles and squares so I will use these two big ones. Then we will sort squares, triangles, then we continue with pattern and I will model it before they go back to their seats.
T: I forgot to put the magnet tape on the bigger shapes so I can put them on the board.
C: Sometimes time is an issue which you gain with experience, but if you forgot the magnet tape what else could you use?
T: Pocket chart.
C: Right.

Not only did the sessions degenerate into dealing with logistical problems rather than focusing on pedagogy or content, but when the coach *was* teaching it was very procedural and didactic. The coaches told the teachers exactly what to do, "start with a human pattern," "stick with the same order," and even gave the teachers step-by-step instructions, "then we will sort," "then we continue with the pattern." The teachers were given a procedure to use rather than being led to pedagogical self-discovery. They were taught to carry out an activity but not given the pedagogical or mathematical understanding to value the activity (e.g. what students are thinking during these activities and why the activity promotes students' conceptual discovery). These examples bear striking resemblance to the example shown earlier where students are taught how to solve an equation but are not provided opportunities for developing conceptual understanding. Since teachers are not led through self-discovery of pedagogy, they are denied the tools of critical thinking which could make them self-evolving, independent thinkers in regards to their pedagogy.

Besides mathematics coaching, the MIG and PA are two key instructional tools that in theory should support mathematics teaching and learning. In practice, however, these instructional tools are primarily used to drive teaching and learning towards state accountability tests.

Math Instructional Guide (MIG)

The MIG details the different standards for each quarter, yet it is not a true guide because it does not describe the connection between the concepts and the standards, and the underlying big ideas that connect different standards and concepts. The MIG is also structured so that teaching is driven by the PAs and, ultimately, the state's content standards tests. Periodic assessments are not used as a diagnostic tool because assessment results are not being used to inform instruction; if they are, it is at a very superficial level where administrators and teachers simply look at the students' weaknesses and strengths for reteaching (i.e., repeating teaching a concept in the same way even though the approach has not been effective as evident in students' assessment results). The support teachers receive tend to focus on the operational aspects of the MIG and PAs.

MIG: Use, Impact, and Support System

When asked to describe the ways in which they applied the MIG in their teaching of mathematics, the majority of the teachers reported using the MIG as a general guideline to help plan instruction for the quarter and to choose what content to focus on (67% of elementary and 51% of secondary). Some teachers, however, indicated that they either do not understand the term "Math Instructional Guide", or do not use the MIG at all, or that they use the MIG as a directive and a "tool" to prepare students for the test. The MIG is not used as a tool for conceptual development of students or toward qualitative improvement of instruction (i.e., focusing on big mathematical ideas, or emphasizing connections among different concepts and standards).

Discrepancies in the application of the MIG could begin at the most fundamental level with teachers (27%)[4] not recognizing the term "Math Instructional Guide". The following responses are typical illustrations of these teachers' confusion about the term MIG.

Q:[5] Now I'd like to ask you about the Math Instructional Guide. What types of support are you receiving on the Math Instructional Guide this school year?

T: I don't really understand what you're talking about, Math Instructional Guide.

Q: Now I'd like to ask you about the Math Instructional Guide.

T: You mean the standards, or do you mean this thing? Oh you mean something else, okay that thing. Okay, I think I know what you mean.

Q: Can you show me what you typically think of as your Math Instructional Guide?

T: I call it the math book.

Q: That's your teachers' guide to your textbook, your Harcourt textbook.

T: That's what I use mostly.

Q: Okay, so let me qualify that then. I'd like to ask you about what used to be called the pacing plan.

Most teachers who were given clarification on the terminology were able to respond appropriately to our questions related to the MIG, showing that unfamiliarity with the term did not necessarily constitute unfamiliarity with the document itself. However, the fact that some teachers misunderstood the terminology cannot be regarded as insignificant. A discrepancy in the nomenclature of a significant tool is quite troubling and is indicative of a larger disconnection in communication between the producers of the MIG and its consumers, that is, teachers.

About 23%[6] of elementary teachers (only 8% of secondary teachers) gave responses that focused on using the MIG as a guide to cover the content that will be on the PAs so that students are prepared for these assessments.

T1: Well I follow the pacing schedule so that I am prepared for the assessments. If not then the children are faced with math skills that they aren't familiar with and it's frustrating to them.
T2: Well, in Algebra 1, I used the Pacing Plan to prepare them for the quarterly assessments. And that's about it.

The concerns expressed in these responses centered on test preparation instead of mathematical understanding or conceptual development of students.

Additionally, teachers' responses suggest that the MIG is used as a directive rather than as an aide to qualitative improvement of instruction. About 8% of elementary teachers and 12% of secondary teachers reported that they follow both the sequence and timing outlined in the MIG to cover content for each quarter of the semester. Their typical responses are as follows:

T1: Basically they give it to us and tell us we have to stick to it, and I have.
T2: Well, I follow it to the letter. I cover every section they say, in the order they say.
T3: Really we follow just the guidelines, the state standards that we have to follow now. We are compelled to do that. And you follow the standards. You follow what is required for you to teach them I suppose.

These responses indicate a conceptualization of the MIG as a directive complete with an anonymous "they" giving orders in the phrases, "they... tell us" or "they say." This sense of "following orders" is heightened with the phrases such as "we are compelled" or "follow what is required." At no point did teachers mention the MIG as a tool that serves them and offers assistance for qualitative improvement of instruction, but rather as a directive that demands to be followed.

Teachers expressed various concerns with the MIG. Close to one-third (29%) of secondary teachers (but only 2% of elementary teachers) reported not using the MIG at all or attempting to follow the MIG but falling behind. The most common reason given for not using the MIG, particularly at the secondary level, is that students' lagging in their mathematical development makes it difficult or impossible to teach grade level content at the pace required by the MIG.

T1: I have applied it, but I usually can't follow long with it because it takes a while for the students to understand some of the concepts we go over. It happens to be that when we first start on it, it works out great, but as the material starts getting difficult, I tend to slow down a little more, just so that they can get the topics we're going over and so that they can feel comfortable. I tend to follow it for a certain amount of time and then just happen to pass me up.

T2: I mean, you want to try to cover everything that they want in the Math Instructional Guide, but with the level of students, it's not always possible.

To summarize, though teachers gave different responses on the way that they use the MIG, analysis of their responses suggested some common themes in the way the MIG is applied. Specifically, the MIG is not used as a tool that provides assistance in improving instruction, but rather as a document that demands to be adhered to. The only change in instruction is that certain content is covered, but there is no indication of a qualitative difference in the way such content is covered. Furthermore, the ultimate purpose of this directive is to prepare students for the PA instead of helping students evolve conceptually in mathematics. At no time in their responses did teachers give any indication that the MIG is used or applied in a way that aides in furthering students' mathematical conceptual development or improving teachers' instructional practices. The use of the MIG centered on following orders and driving instruction toward the PAs.

The teachers' reported use of the MIG correlates strongly with the support that teachers indicate receiving. Eighteen percent of the teachers reported receiving no support on the MIG at all while another 32% reported that support on the MIG was limited to supplies and instructional materials. For the reminder of the teachers, 40% of them attended training in a trainer-led group setting. Only 5% reported any one-on-one training with the mathematics coach and another 5% claimed that their colleagues are their only available support.

Teachers' impressions of the term "support" is also revealing. For instance, when asked what types of support they found most useful, many teachers (32%) gave answers that indicated an unusual interpretation of the word "support" or indicated self-support.

T1: Well, I find the dates are useful, and also they describe the power standards that you need to actually cover. And also—they describe what sections of your math textbook you may use to support that area.

T2: Well it's the sequence of the lessons, the way it's planned out, so that helps me a lot in getting my lessons, preparing for my lessons.

T3: When you say the Math Instructional Guide, you're referring to the pacing plan? [Exactly.] I mean, it's good to know the key standards, so as we go through, I don't, I really don't, like the pace that it's at.

As evidenced in these quotes, when teachers were asked about support on using the MIG, their responses focus on the MIG itself. In other words, elements of the document itself (e.g., "power standards") or the teacher's use of the document (e.g., "preparing for my lessons") is seen as the best support. It seems teachers' experience of "support" does not include external sources or collegial influences.

Interviews of mathematics coaches, school administrators (i.e., principals or assistant principals), and mathematics department chairs indicated that for the most part coaches and the administrators at schools provided only superficial support to their teachers. Similar to the teacher interviews, there was an unclear understanding of the word "support". Thirty-four percent of the time the coaches' and administrators' responses to the question centered around logistics, or observing classes, but they did not discuss how they are supporting teachers with the MIG. About 10% of the coaches and administrators reported providing no support for the MIG, while 42% of the coaches and administrators stated they discussed the MIG with teachers. Discussions usually mean going through the information in the MIG, creating a calendar with a schedule of the numbers of days teachers will spend on a lesson or standard, and showing teachers where the alternative resources are located. For instance, a typical discussion by coaches or administrators would be:

> I'll usually write out a pacing plan for them. Then we'll try to get together if I don't get a chance to meet with the entire grade level. Then I'll talk to someone within the grade level and they'll have a chance to look over it and make adjustments and whatever. But I try to give them an outline first of all

the standards and the concepts and everything that's going to be covered for the assessment period, and resources that they can use and different supplemental and things like that.

The support provided in such a manner is at a superficial level, as they only determine what is the best content to cover and the best time to cover it. Different strategies and alternative resources may be mentioned or listed (as these resources are in the MIG), but are not elaborated or discussed. Six percent of the time the coaches or administrators simply provide or hand materials from the MIG to the teachers. There is no explanation of what the MIG is, what its purpose is and how the teachers are supposed to use it. Sometimes the coach would provide a calendar with the standards and lessons laid out for the teachers, but there was no indication that a meeting took place to discuss the calendar, why it was laid out the way it was or what strategies could be used to teach the lessons effectively. A typical example of this kind of support is as follows:

> At the beginning of every quarter I give them another copy of the blueprint and I also gave them a calendar with the daily blocks on it that cover the pages and the standards, so they can get through all the materials.

Elaboration and discussion of different resources and alternative strategies happens only 8% of the time. Coaches take these meetings a step further and have the teachers discuss how they can use the alternative resources and teaching strategies in their classrooms. They may do a sample lesson and discuss what was good about it, what concept it covered, and what teachers can apply to their individual classrooms.

Although these discussions are more aligned with the intended use of the MIG, the focus is not to enhance students' mathematical learning but to address the concepts and standards that will be tested that quarter.

Not surprisingly, classroom observations suggest that the MIG does not have much impact on the way teachers approach their lessons, whether they use the MIG or not.

About 18% of all teachers (both elementary and secondary) did not consider the MIG worth utilizing. Based on answers that teachers gave, most of them see the MIG as a guideline telling them what they need to cover—not as a tool to help them improve their teaching. But about 59% of teachers did see some use in the MIG and have chosen to use it in some way. Their answers indicate, however, that they view the MIG much in the same way as all other teachers—as a guideline for what needs to be covered in preparation for the test.

These findings of teaching to the test and the lack of support are also seen in direct observations of school site professional development. Observations show that the discussion surrounding the MIG is generally concerned with figuring out how many days to spend on a concept in order to cover all concepts listed in the MIG as can be seen in the following:

C: OK, quarter 3 has 48 days, the 49th day is your CRT, the 50th day is multiple-choice and day 51 is scoring. So I want you to do the pacing plan for me: the standards and pages for each day.

T1: Can we use some of those days for review when we come back on track?

C: Yes, there are enough days, use the first day or two for review. Here is the instructional guide. Make sure you get the correct standard.

T1: Sixteen standards, 48 days, that's three days per standard

C: Figure out the standards and page numbers you need to hit every day.
[Teachers count number of days within a quarter to the number of lessons needed to be taught as aligned by the MIG.]

T1: Let's write down the math pacing in our lesson planners. Qtr. 1, we have Mon–Wed with scores entered by Wed…. Let's count lessons and fit those into the days. Testing for Qtr 2 is… [Teacher counts the days in her calendar.] I'm getting 53 days.

T2: Me too.

T3: Monday, you have to take your time, there's lots to cover….

T1: We are going to compact lessons because there are more than 54 lessons…53 days, but 55, plus supplemental….

T4: Why don't we just do one concept a day?

T1: It depends on what they need.

T4: Are you doing any other assessments during this time?

T2: I do chapter tests and there are also unit tests.

In other words, the focus is on "Let's count lessons and fit those into the days," without the incorporation of deeper learning. There is little inclusion of the idea of "chunking" standards together, which might give teachers more time to teach a concept.

The concern with having enough time to cover all concepts listed in the MIG seems to be driven by the district periodic assessments (PA).

T1: T2 has such a small class, she is able to pull out resource material, try it and then share it with us. We've agreed that the "Swiss cheese" way the district has mandated us to do math is working—our scores have gone up.

T1: This was (the) unit opener.
I still don't know how to use this.
I'm thinking…some of this stuff is subjective.
[After C responds.] So we should collect these for the kids [the Inquiry Journals].

T2: The Abacus.

T1: But that won't help me for the test.

T2: Teach to the test?

T1: As much as you can, I do. If they're not giving us enough time to teach the material!

Teachers' focus on driving instruction towards the PA is a reflection of the test-driven culture seen in direct observations at the central and local district PD training. At the elementary level, 62% of the MIG training consisted of revision of the elementary MIG in order to ensure topics assessed by the PA during a particular quarter are covered. This concern was observed in the majority of the MIG training throughout the school year.

At the secondary level, 50% of the MIG training involves grouping standards. Grouping standards or "chunking standards" has the potential for promoting the "Big Ideas" of the MIG. It is not clear, however, how much value or emphasis teachers may place on "Big Ideas". The following is the "share out" time of a Grouping Standards activity:

T: We came up with a flow chart and grouped the standards into clusters.
This is [the] geometric part. We have a cube, fraction, decimals; basically we had all standards tied together. The idea to connect geometry related to this. We wanted to keep it simple because these are the skills that we need to know.

MF:[7] The reasoning standards are at the bottom.

T: Those must have not been tied to the big thing.

MF: I thought you did that because it was going to be the support for everything. [Teachers laugh.]

It can be seen that the teacher's groupings were based on skills and not on the mathematical concepts contained in the standards. The fact that the reasoning standards were seen as not being "tied to the big thing" speaks volumes that there is not a clear, concise understanding of the conceptual nature of the "Big Ideas."

To summarize, though teachers give different responses in the way that they use the MIG, analysis of their responses suggests some common themes in the way the MIG is applied. Specifically, the MIG is not used as a tool that provides assistance in improving instruction, but rather as a document that demands to be adhered to. The only change in instruction is that certain content is covered, but there is no indication of a qualitative difference in the way such content is covered. Furthermore, the ultimate purpose of this directive is to prepare students for the PA instead of helping students evolve conceptually in mathematics. At no time in their responses do teachers give any indication that the MIG is used or applied in a way that aids in furthering students' mathematical conceptual development or improving teachers' instructional practices. The focus of the use of MIG centers on following a district mandate and driving instruction toward the PAs.

PERIODIC ASSESSMENTS: USE, IMPACT, AND SUPPORT SYSTEM

Most teachers (elementary 63%, secondary 39%) reported using the results for some form of remediation for students. Typically, these teachers reported that they analyzed results to find students' strengths and weaknesses. Teachers then reteach content areas where students' performance was low. Teachers may reteach in small groups or as a whole class. Teachers may review the test, give students similar items to practice, give particular students extra homework, or have warm-ups focused on reviewing content. While review can be helpful, these teachers give no indication that they are reteaching any differently. Our classroom observations indicate a dominant procedural approach to mathematics teaching and learning. If the problem is that teachers did not teach in a way that facilitates conceptual understanding in the first place, then repeating the same lesson will still not promote conceptual understanding, even if such reteaching may familiarize the students with a particular procedure. In this sense, the use of the data is superficial, not making any real change to student learning or instructional practice.

There were also a number of teachers (elementary, 14%; secondary, 22%) who reported using the results for other purposes. These teachers may incorporate results into students' grades, award bonus points, or provide other incentives for students to do well on the test. They may share results with students or parents, discuss the results at a grade level or staff meeting, or use the results to group students in the classroom. Using PA results in these ways has an even lesser impact on students' actual learning and conceptual development.

Furthermore, some teachers (elementary, 9%; secondary, 33%) reported doing little or nothing with the PA results. Teachers reported that they may "look at" the results or simply discard them. Teachers cited various reasons for not using the results, the most common one being a lack of confidence in the validity of the test results. At the elementary level, teachers reported a lack of confidence because "the language of the test is not appropriate" or because they felt the test was "unfair." At the secondary level, teachers who considered test results as invalid often reported that they were unable to cover the content before the test, and that students did not "take the test seriously." Some teachers reported that assessment results were not received in a timely manner or not received at all. Others reported that taking time to review would only cause them to fall further behind in the pacing plan (a complaint also lodged by those teachers who *did* review). Regardless of the reasons, this use of the PA is clearly of no advantage.

Finally, some teachers (elementary, 14%; secondary, 6%) reported using the results to evaluate and/or make changes to teaching practices. Teachers may seek out new strategies for teaching certain content or simply make teaching notes for next year (e.g., to spend more time on a certain topic). Spending more time on a certain topic does not imply any qualitative instructional changes and therefore does not foreshadow any change in students' actual conceptual development. However, using data to modify instructional practices, as the following teacher indicated, could have implications for student learning:

T: Well, I look for patterns and see if it's something that most of them got wrong. I obviously did something in my delivery of my lesson.

Using data to evaluate details of instructional practices and make changes could potentially deliver a higher level of students' conceptual understanding. While this is excellent in theory, we will need to look into what "alternative strategies" teachers are learning and what the effect of "sharing practices" is. For instance, if "alternative strategies" are no more pedagogically advanced than current strategies, or if "sharing practices" consists of teachers' sharing practices that are procedural rather than conceptual, this could make little difference. Still, these teachers represent those who are beginning to show a more critical and meaningful use of the data—analyzing data toward change in instructional practices.

To summarize, most teachers used results minimally or not at all, or used results in a superficial application of the data, and only a small percentage of teachers applied the data in a way that has potential for producing significant change. The teachers' use of the PA results is revealing, but it cannot be studied in isolation. To properly contextualize this information, we must turn to the larger system in which teachers are operating and examine the support system under which teachers work.

The cultural view of the PAs, as illustrated by the kind of support that is given, is consistent with how teachers approach the PAs and use assessment results. Teachers reported that the support they received on the PAs is largely logistical (e.g., scanning answer sheets) and preparatory (helping teachers prepare students for the test). Relatively little weight is given to supporting teachers in analyzing the results of the assessments. At the elementary school level, only 12% of teachers were given support in analyzing their data even at a superficial level (we call this level 1 analysis, namely analyzing for students' strengths and weaknesses in order to reteach). Only 1% of the teachers were supported in more purposeful analysis (we call this level 2 analysis, namely analyzing for students' strengths and weaknesses in order to make pedagogical alterations). At the secondary level, only 6% were supported in level 1 analysis, and none were supported in level 2 analysis.

Teachers reported that support for the PA is focused on taking the test and not on post-test analysis, and to an even lesser extent toward analyzing data in order to improve instruction.

These findings are also consistent with the findings from interviews of mathematics coaches, principals/assistant principals, and mathematics department chairs. Most coaches and administrators (49%) recognized that a function of the PA results was to reveal the strengths and weaknesses of a particular teacher's class for the purpose of review or reteaching for the next PA (level 1 analysis). Here is an example of what was reported as typical support for teachers:

C: We look at the standards which they performed better in, and what they performed, what they were weaker in.

It can be seen that there is limited use of the PA results. An additional 8% of the coaches and administrators reported that they did not do anything with the PA results, because they did not believe the results were worth looking into, or the results did not reflect an actual or fair assessment of their students' mathematical skills. There was also a small number (4%) of administrators who reported merely handing the results to their teachers. Although the results are being distributed there is no way to determine how those results are actually being used.

Examination of the leadership interview data provided additional insights on the intended versus actual use of the PA results. The mathematics leadership team was asked how the PA was intended to be used and how it was actually being used. Eighty-one percent of the interviewees reported at least one intended use of the PAs. The top intended uses of the PAs, according to the mathematics leadership team, are as follows: inform or drive instruction (47%), used as a diagnostic tool (27%), used for reteaching (10%), and used to help teachers collaborate (10%). When asked about actual use of the PAs, only 3% reported the PAs being used as intended—to inform or drive instruction. The most prominent use (50%) of the PAs that was reported was its use as an evaluative tool, or high stakes test. The following are examples of the way the PA results are being misused:

Administrator 1:   I also wanted to add to that, that many administrators are using the math assessments to evaluate teachers, and I have heard stories of administrators calling in teachers saying, "Hey, you know what, your last quarter two math scores were pretty low compared to Mrs. So and So down the hall and you got the same kind of kids. What's going on here?" That's not the purpose. I think it(s) got to be made very clear to the administrators that it is for the teachers, or themselves, but it's simply formative for them.

Administrator 2:   It's not a high stakes test like the CST, the CAT6, it's just we're going to look at it, we're going to change our instructional approach.

Administrator 3:   I want to say yes because—well, I'm going to say yes, because sometimes the data is being used as an evaluation and not just as a formative tool. I think some teachers don't want these results shared with administrators for possible, you know, reflection on them if it's not as good as it should be. I think that's about the only thing.

The misuse of the PAs as an evaluative tool could help explain why there has not been a complete "buy in" from teachers.

As discussed previously, the PAs are not intended as an accountability tool; their intended use is as a low stakes diagnostic tool, whose results are used to inform instruction and therefore improve instructional practices. The view that even though the PAs are not used for their intended purposes, they at least keep teachers on track, can be seen in the following excerpts:

Administrator 1:   All the teachers have a focus per quarter of what they should be teaching because accountability is via the periodic assessment, and there's a good correlation between the periodic assessment and the CST in terms of performance.

Administrator 2:   Force teachers to use MIG and teach what's in the MIG since periodic assessment is holding teachers accountable.

Twenty-seven percent of the leadership stated that the PAs had improved instruction by making teachers cover the content in order to prepare students for the high stakes state standards tests. In other words, even though PAs are not used as intended (i.e., low stakes and diagnostic for the purpose of improving instruction), they at least ensure that the teachers are covering the material that is going to appear on the state standardized tests. The PA is also seen as improving instruction because it forces teachers to teach areas that they are not comfortable with or that the students do not understand. This is evident in the following example:

Another piece of it is that, whereas, before in some cases, if a teacher was teaching mathematics, if the class didn't get a particular concept, it's like they got stuck on that concept. And so at one of the schools I personally worked with there was, I know at least a couple of teachers, where they only got to Chapter 4 in a year. Whereas, now, you know, perhaps they're not covering—well, perhaps that's all they're doing, "covering" the material... [But at least they're covering material.] But at least there is some exposure for the students. [If it's not in-depth, at least it's...] At least it's, you know, something.

Classroom observations show that when teachers view the results of the PA as a gauge of where their students need improving, they take that information and just reteach, in the same procedural fashion, in the areas that their students need help. Teachers are not making the connection between the PA results and how they can improve their teaching practices to be more conceptual.

There is a distinct difference between the elementary and secondary levels in how they utilize PA results. At the elementary level, teachers utilize the results 63% of the time while secondary teachers utilize them 36% of the time. Almost half (42%) of all secondary teachers barely took notice of the results, claiming that they knew the students would do poorly anyway or their students did not try on the test so there was no reason to bother with the results. This limited use of the PA results is also seen in direct observation at school site PD.

The PD that is provided on the school site involves many conversations centered around instruction and test results. These discussions had more to do with reviewing and comparing "numbers" as opposed to any in-depth conversations about how to use test results to inform instruction. This level 1 analysis (i.e., using PA results at a superficial level) was reported throughout in interviews and is obvious in the following faculty meeting led by the mathematics coach:

C: We're here today to talk about the Qtr. 2 assessment, Qtr. 3 and activities for Qtr 3. I'm going to guide you through your data.
[C puts an example of the quarterly assessment data on the OHP. It is a dense chart of numbers and the observer was not able to copy it down.]

C: If you look up here, this is your class average.... On this printout, which shall remain nameless, you can see that 17.1 out of 34, so ½ or 50% of the kids are strategic...standard 3.2 was questions 20, 27 ...and so on....Okay turn it over and you will see the results for question 20.   [C puts up a new transparency on the OHP.] These bars are an easy way to look at performance.

T: I got zero %. Is that possible?

C: Yes, that means nobody got it right. What's the next one you want to look at?

T: When can I have time to revisit and review the problems?

C: Okay, one way to do it is to review for 5 minutes at the start of each lesson...give them three practice problems at the start of the class.

The statement, "you can see that 17.1 out of 34, so ½ or 50% of the kids are strategic... standard 3.2 was questions 20, 27 ...and so on," reflects the superficial approach and lack of detailed breakdown of information that the coach is delivering to the teachers. "I got zero %. Is that possible?" "Yes, that means nobody got it right. What's the next one you want to look at?" Rather than focus on the specifics of the teacher's issue and use it to model for further, deeper investigation, the coach chooses to move on. "When can I have time to revisit and review the problems?" "OK, one way to do it is to review for 5 minutes at the start of each lesson...give them three practice problems at the start of the class." The coach's solution for the teacher is procedural, computational repetition. This is level 1 data analysis where there is no discussion about how the teacher could change their teaching strategy to reteach the concepts. These findings are not limited to school site professional development; they are also seen at local district and central district training.

Professional development at the district levels for the MIG and PA included discussions, workshops, activities, training, and work meetings. The majority (92% at the secondary level and 72% at the elementary level) was embedded in other formal training. Only 8% (at the secondary level) and 28% (at the elementary level) were not embedded and of this training at the elementary level, all included revision of the EMIG (Elementary Math Instructional Guide). Leadership interviews revealed that formal training for the MIG and/or PAs were not provided. The time range for the embedded training was from 1–105 minutes. This assortment of events will be referred to as "training" hereafter.

At the elementary level, 60% of the PA training consisted of dealing with logistics, including PA testing dates, technical difficulties with the assessment software (scanning and password), and PA delivery and distribution. Over half of the training of the PA is purely logistical and deals with problem solving and this is reflective in the support received by teachers in which logistics and preparation support was the majority of support received. Twenty percent of the PA training involved data analysis, however, the training was all superficial and only included level 1 analysis. The remaining training consisted of 10% assessment software program training and 10% related to the PAs.

At the secondary level, 73% of the PA training involved activities using PA questions for familiarity or to correlate with MIG standards; 28% involved relating past PA questions to the standards they address; 27% addressed the rigor of PA questions; while 18% consisted of looking at former PA questions for familiarity. Only 9% of the training involved data analysis. Yet this training, like elementary school, consisted solely of superficial data analysis. The following is an excerpt from data analysis training:

F:[8] (The) second part is the item analysis...last year we tried to match it up with the rational sheet to see where we needed reteaching. Behind (that) is the Performance Band report. How does it differ from the test detail...the percentages are different.

T: The number of students that are below 50%.

F: See how many in what band (are) intensive, strategic, and benchmark...this at the bottom is very important, how many kids are 50% or below. What are we going to do, how do we remedy this? How do we figure out how to reteach? Next one is a new report that's extremely valuable...when you sign on look for "item analysis"...you can get detailed information school wide.

[The conversation digressed to complaints about the PA questions.]

This exchange is indicative of a superficial, level 1 analysis of the PA data. The question "How do we figure out how to reteach?" was asked, although it did not result in an in-depth conversation about how to reteach and what contributed to the low scores. The data analysis simply consisted of looking at the numbers and asking questions, yet it did not result in how to remedy the problems of low test scores and how to implement these remedies at school sites.

These findings show that the central and local district training given for the periodic assessment is focused primarily on taking the test and not on improving instruction through post-test analysis. As we have seen in the teacher interviews, the use of the PAs is very test-driven and at the central and local district level this cultural view remains the same.

Although the majority of PA use is superficial there were a limited number of administrators who reported that they supported teachers to help teachers improve their teaching practices (level 2 analysis). Thirteen math coaches or administrators stated that they help their teachers collaborate and discuss the different teaching methods they use to teach particular areas. For example, if the PA results reveal that one teacher was strong in teaching about number sense, but all the others seemed to not be doing something right, that teacher would share with all the other teachers how he or she taught the concept so that the others would have an idea of how to improve their own teaching. Some examples of these answers were:

> Then we talk about standards that we know we need to reteach as a grade level, then standards you need to reteach or have some kind of remediation and just in your classroom. Then we talk about how you taught those things, and how we could not do it louder and slower, but how we can do it in a different way so that the kids have access to it, because obviously what we did that quarter didn't work.
>
> What we do is once they analyze the data, we spend considerable time in common planning to take the analysis of the data and do demonstration lessons so that teachers can observe their colleagues to see what kind of lessons are created based upon those assessments. So if teachers have looked at comparative data and found that their children have done better in one area, then we allow those teachers to demonstrate those model lessons to their colleagues so that they may incorporate some of those strategies into their class.

The collaboration between teachers and use of the PA results to change teacher instruction is a great example of how the PA was intended to improve instruction. The question is: Why are there so few teachers and administrators who use the PA as it was intended?

The support system provided to teachers on the MIG and PA provides a larger context and is an appropriate arena to examine characteristics of the system's culture as a whole. Examining the support given to teachers reveals that teachers' use of the MIG/PA is merely symptomatic of the system's culture at large. In other words, the system's culture generally does not exhibit a drive toward improving instructional practices or a concern for students' conceptual development, but rather is driven towards test-taking.

To summarize, 39% of teachers use results minimally or not at all, 51% use results in a superficial application of the data, and only 10% apply the data in a way that has potential for producing significant change. This limited ways of using of the PA test results are disappointing, but it is even more unsettling given the fact that the efforts to apply the MIG are geared toward the PA and yet the potential benefits of using the PA test results to improve instruction are not utilized.

GOOD INTENTION, MISPLACED EMPHASIS

The district's reform effort discussed in this chapter reveals a few lessons. In theory, coaching support in terms of providing one-on-one demonstration lessons holds promise for teachers' development of both content and pedagogy. Examination of the quality of this training, however, showed that it did not help to develop teachers' mathematical conceptual understanding. The training focused more on the "how" rather than the "why."

Furthermore, MIG and PA are two important instructional tools the district implemented to further support teachers. Their use in practice, however, showed that these tools were used to drive mathematics teaching and learning towards testing instead of being used as tools for improving instruction. It is not surprising then that the district effort as a whole had little impact on the way in which teachers engage students about substantive mathematics when they come together in classrooms. The bottom line is that anchoring a reform effort around testing and accountability, instead of continuous growth of teachers' knowledge and skill, worked against what the reform aims to accomplish. This theme will be highlighted in Chap. 6 and discussed further in Chap. 7.

Teachers play a central role in determining what is taught and learned in schools, and how it is taught, a role no curriculum by itself can fulfill (Shulman 1986; Stigler and Hiebert 1999). While the focus on alternative teaching strategies, such as using manipulatives, in theory sounds good, developing teachers' knowledge of mathematics for the purpose of teaching cannot be solely accomplished by modeling without making explicit the connection between the mathematical concepts or big ideas (not just a list of standards) and the tools (i.e., manipulatives, MIG, or PAs).Teaching is not a sequence of behaviors (i.e., scripting each step of the way asking teachers what to say or to do) and the essence of mathematics is not about following steps or procedures, but problem solving and thinking, which does not always follow prescribed steps.

NOTES

1. The MIG does not provide detailed sequencing or pacing of the content standards for each quarter. Rather, the MIG only lists the standards to be covered for that quarter.
2. C: math coach; S: a student; Ss: students; T: teacher; GH: Hispanic girl; BH: Hispanic boy.
3. They refer to the students. Here the coach is telling teachers what to do, what to say, what students know, etc.
4. After realizing that many teachers were unclear regarding the terminology, interviewers added a clarifying clause to the question (e.g. "the document formerly known as the pacing plan"). Teachers who were given this initial clarification are not counted in this statistic.
5. Q: questioner.
6. Statistics regarding the use of the MIG do not include teachers who continued to discuss something other than the MIG (e.g., the textbook) when describing their MIG use.
7. MF: math facilitator.
8. F: facilitator.

REFERENCES

Ball, D., & Rowan, B. (2004). Introduction: Measuring instruction. *The Elementary School Journal, 105*(1), 3–10.

Cohen, D., & Ball, D. (2001, September). Making change: Instruction and its improvement. *A Kappan Special Section on School Reform.*

Hill, H., & Ball, D. (2004). Learning mathematics for teaching: Results from California's Mathematics Professional Development Institutes. *Journal for Research in Mathematics Education, 35*(5), 330–351.

Ma, L. (1999). *Knowing and teaching elementary mathematics: Teachers' understanding of fundamental mathematics in China and the United States.* Mahwah: Lawrence Erlbaum Associates.

Ma, L. (2010). *Knowing and teaching elementary mathematics: Teachers' understanding of fundamental mathematics in China and the United States* (2nd ed.). New York: Routledge.

Shulman, L. (1986). Those who understand: Knowledge growth in teaching. *Educational Researcher, 15*, 4–14.

Stigler, J., & Hiebert, J. (1999). *The teaching gap: Best ideas from the world's teachers for improving education in the classroom.* New York: The Free Press.

CHAPTER 6

Conceptual Understanding of Foundational Mathematical Topics: What Might They Look Like?

Conceptual understanding is a buzzword among the mathematics education community. But what does conceptual understanding mean when we focus on a particular mathematical topic or concept? What differentiates conceptual understanding from fragile understanding? This chapter attempts to answer these questions through illustrating what in-depth understanding of several foundational mathematical topics might look like.

In the sections that follow, I will first describe an anecdote. Then I will discuss two major criteria and a framework that outlines central characteristics exemplified in mathematical conceptual understanding. I developed this framework with one of my former doctoral advisees based on prior scholars' work on mathematical content understanding. After this I will describe how these characteristics manifest themselves in specific topics (e.g., what does conceptual understanding look like when we think about the concept of place value?). This chapter is foundational in terms of setting a benchmark against the kind of understanding that teachers are exposed to which can be characterized as fragmented, incoherent, and superficial.

An Anecdote

To illustrate what conceptual understanding of mathematics means, perhaps it is better to begin with an example that is the opposite of conceptual understanding. At the National Math Panel (NMP) public hearing referred to in the Preface of this book, one of the public speakers gave an example

© The Author(s) 2018
X. A. Newton, *Improving Teacher Knowledge in K-12 Schooling*,
https://doi.org/10.1007/978-3-319-71207-9_6

of what good mathematics teaching and learning (for developing students' conceptual understanding of mathematics) would look like and said something along these lines: "Suppose you are teaching students how to find the sum of interior angles of a [regular] polygon. One approach is to give them the formula and then give them a worksheet to practice the formula. Alternatively, we can have students measure the angles of different polygons and then derive the formula themselves." The presenter intended to show that the former approach (i.e., teachers tell and students practice) is bad, but the alternative approach (i.e., students construct the formula based on hands-on manipulation) is good.

Although the drill and kill approach might not help students understand what they are doing, the alternative approach suggested by the presenter is not that great either in terms of helping students to develop their mathematical understanding. On the contrary, the alternative approach might even send a wrong message to students that mathematical proof is equivalent to showing, via a few examples, that something works in all situations (in this example, the interior angle formula works for all polygons even though students may have "derived" the formula based on observations of only a few examples).

The point is *not* that teachers should not give students a few examples to explore and construct the formula. The point is that after the exploration, teachers will need to help students see why the formula would work for all polygons. This understanding requires that teachers foster students' capacity for constructing rigorous mathematical proofs. This type of mathematical capacity is a manifestation of what mathematical conceptual understanding means. Without such capacity, students will develop what Howard Gardner (1991) calls a "fragile understanding" of school subjects described in his book *Unschooled Mind*, which was nicely summarized by Daniel Gursky (1991) in his *Education Week* report:

> [In the book, Gardner argued that] even in schools with the highest test scores, students who master the material adequately enough to perform well in class and on exams don't really understand what they're being taught. Gardner used a phone conversation with his own daughter to bring the point home. When Kerith—who had done well in high school physics—called from college, distressed about her physics class, Gardner offered some fatherly advice: Don't worry so much about the grade, he told her, just try to understand the material. "You don't get it, Dad," Kerith replied, "I've never understood it." Kerith has plenty of company. Many top students at elite universities exhibit fragile understanding, at best.

Gardner's observation that top students who could perform well in exams do not necessarily understand what they are taught resonates with the research findings on undergraduate STEM majors' understanding of foundational algebra topics such as slope discussed in Chap. 4 of this book. But what does conceptual understanding mean when we focus on a particular mathematical topic or concept? What differentiate conceptual understanding from fragile understanding? The sections that follow provide some perspectives on these two questions.

CRITERIA FOR CONCEPTUAL UNDERSTANDING: TEACH-ABILITY AND MATHEMATICAL INTEGRITY

The criteria for mathematical conceptual understanding described in this section are developed by Hung-Hsi Wu, a mathematician and professor emeritus of the Department of Mathematics at University of California Berkeley. Wu has devoted decades of effort at addressing the issue of mathematics teachers' subject knowledge and is currently finishing his book series delineating the mathematical topics from elementary to high school for teachers, published by the American Mathematical Society (Wu 2011b, 2016a, b).

According to Wu, since K-12 mathematics curriculum is not a proper subset of the mathematics taught in college (Ball et al. 2008; Wu 2006, 2014), the mathematical knowledge teachers need to have must meet two basic requirements. First, such knowledge needs to mirror closely what is taught in K-12 classrooms. Secondly, such knowledge needs to respect the integrity of mathematics. The implication of the first requirement is that teachers will not be able to explain to an elementary student that fractions are equivalence classes of ordered pairs of integers or to a high-school student that slope of a non-vertical line is the first derivative of the linear function that defines that line. These definitions, which are basic concepts in college mathematics, do not make any sense to an elementary student who has no idea what ordered pairs of integers mean or to a high-school student who has yet to learn calculus. In other words, teachers will need to define what a fraction or slope is using language that is understandable by an elementary or a high-school student, respectively.

At the same time, the implication of the second requirement (i.e., maintaining mathematical rigor) is that in the process of making a mathematical concept accessible to students, the *mathematical* meaning of a concept should never get lost (e.g., giving students incorrect and often times confusing information). For instance, when students first encounter the concept of fractions, they are often shown the pictures of pizzas or pies and then are told that fractions are part of a whole, etc. But what does multiplying or dividing pizzas or pies mean? What is the connection between the algorithm of adding, subtracting, multiplying, or dividing fractions and the pizzas/pies? And when Algebra 1 students are first introduced to the concept of slope, they are shown a picture of an airplane taking off, or a person climbing up stairs and then are told that slope is the rise over run. But what has the rise and run in an airplane taking off or someone climbing stairs got to do with numbers when students have to understand that the slope of a line is a *number* associated with the line? Is this really the way we want to teach students the mathematical meaning of slope?

To summarize, the mathematical content knowledge on which conceptual understanding is built must both respect the integrity of mathematics and be understandable and teachable to K-12 students. It is important to emphasize that such an exposition of K-12 mathematics has just begun to receive attention and is being made available in a series of books published by the American Mathematical Society for the first time (Wu 2011b, 2016a, b). Before these books, there were no systematic expositions of K-12 mathematical topics that both satisfy mathematical rigor *and* are teachable to K-12 students. Hence, the kind of content understanding that is foundational for building a coherent conceptual picture of K-12 mathematics was by no means commonplace or available in the mathematics or mathematics education literature until now.

CHARACTERISTICS OF CONCEPTUAL UNDERSTANDING OF MATHEMATICS

To define mathematical conceptual understanding, we need a framework that outlines the central characteristics of content understanding that is teachable to K-12 students while at the same time maintaining the mathematical rigor (i.e., satisfying the two criteria described in the previous section). Based on prior work of mathematicians (e.g., Wu 2010, 2011a, b) and researchers of mathematics education (e.g., Ball et al. 2008; Ma 1999, 2010; Schoenfeld and Kilpatrick 2008), I developed a framework with one of my former doctoral advisees while investigating undergraduate STEM majors' understanding of foundational algebraic topics (Newton and Poon 2015a, b). The following sections review key ideas proposed by prior researchers in order to elaborate our conception of understanding based on prior scholars' work.

WU'S FIVE CHARACTERISTICS

Wu is one of the few mathematicians who have devoted decades of effort at delineating mathematical content knowledge that teachers need to have in order to teach at K-12 level (Wu 2010, 2011b, 2016a, b). Wu (2010, 2011a, b) proposed five basic characteristics capturing the essence of mathematics that is important for K-12 mathematics teaching:

- Precision: Mathematical statements are clear and unambiguous. At any moment, it is clear what is known and what is not known.
- Definitions: They are the bedrock of the mathematical structure. They are the platform that supports reasoning. No definitions, no mathematics.
- Reasoning: The lifeblood of mathematics. The engine that drives problem solving. Its absence is the root cause of teaching and learning by rote.
- Coherence: Mathematics is a tapestry in which all the concepts and skills are interwoven. It is all of a piece.
- Purposefulness: Mathematics is goal-oriented, and every concept or skill is there for a purpose. Mathematics is not just fun and games.

One point worth mentioning is that "purposefulness" in Wu's lists refers to the *mathematical* purpose. For instance, the purpose of defining the slope of a line is to be able to distinguish among all the lines that pass through a fixed point. The purpose of analyzing the graph of a quadratic function is to be able to use the graph to understand the quadratic function itself, in the same way that the graph of linear functions (i.e., a line) help us understand the linear function itself.

In our framework (see Table 6.1), we argue that the mathematical purpose of a definition or a skill could be used to think through the pedagogical purpose of different activities (i.e., orchestrating class activities in such a way that they scaffold students' development of mathematical ideas). For example, when teaching fraction division, start with activities that activate students' prior knowledge of whole number division before diving into activities that involve fraction division. Therefore, the purposefulness in our framework integrates the mathematical and pedagogical purposes into one. In other words, the purposefulness in our framework refers to the means (pedagogical concerns) towards an end (developing mathematical content understanding) line of thinking.

Table 6.1   Characteristics exemplify mathematical content understanding

Characteristics	Descriptions	Link to other scholars' ideas
Precision	Be explicit about precise definitions (e.g., use definitions as a basis for logical reasoning); Pay attention to precise statements (e.g., present mathematical ideas clearly)	Wu (2010, 2011a, b): precision; definition; reasoning Ball (1990): possessing correct knowledge of concepts and procedures; understanding the nature of mathematical knowledge and mathematics as a field (e.g., what establishes the validity of an answer?)
Coherence	Demonstrate the logical interconnectedness of mathematical ideas (e.g., show the logical underpinnings of the algebraic and geometric representations of a mathematical concept and idea, where appropriate); Show logical/sequential progression of mathematical ideas (e.g., show a deliberate effort at scaffolding mathematical ideas from simple to complex, specific to general)	Wu (2010, 2011a, b): coherence; purposefulness Ball (1990): knowing the connections among mathematical ideas Ma (1999, 2010): connectedness; multiple representations; longitudinal coherence Schoenfeld and Kilpatrick (2008): breadth; depth
Purposefulness	Emphasize key or big mathematical ideas; Provide rationale for why key mathematical ideas are relevant to the teaching of a particular mathematical topic at hand; Scaffold students' learning (pedagogical purposefulness) around the mathematical purposefulness	Wu (2010, 2011a, 2011b): purposefulness; reasoning Ball (1990): understanding the underlying principles and meanings Ma (1999, 2010): basic ideas Schoenfeld and Kilpatrick (2008): breadth

MATHEMATICS EDUCATION RESEARCHERS' WORK ON CONTENT UNDERSTANDING

Mathematics educators' and researchers' work on content understanding can be traced back to Lee Shulman. In his 1985 presidential address at the annual meeting of the American Educational Research Association, Lee Shulman (1986) described content as "the missing paradigm" in research on teaching. To address this "missing paradigm" on teaching, Shulman proposed several types of knowledge teachers need in order to teach. One critical type of knowledge is "pedagogical content knowledge" (PCK), which he defined as "the ways of representing and formulating the subject that make it comprehensible to others" (p. 9). Since then, educational scholars have attempted to elaborate what PCK may entail and link it to student learning (e.g., Ball 1990; Ball et al. 2005, 2008; Baumert et al. 2010; Schoenfeld and Kilpatrick 2008).

One theoretical framework of proficiency in teaching mathematics came from Schoenfeld and Kilpatrick (2008). Their framework consists of several dimensions, the first dimension being "knowing school mathematic in depth and breadth" (p. 2). Schoenfeld and Kilpatrick (2008) argue that proficient teachers' knowledge of school mathematics is both broad and deep. The breadth focuses on teachers' ability to have multiple ways of conceptualizing the content, represent the content in various ways, understand key mathematical ideas, and make connections among mathematical topics. The depth, on the other hand, refers to teachers' understanding of how the mathematical ideas grow conceptually from one grade to another. With knowledge that is both broad and deep, teachers will be able to prioritize and organize content focusing on big mathematical ideas and to respond flexibly to students' questions (Schoenfeld and Kilpatrick 2008).

The characteristics of content understanding outlined in Schoenfeld and Kilpatrick's framework are similar to the ideas rooted in a series of work by Deborah Ball and her colleagues (Ball 1990; Ball et al. 2005, 2008) and to those outlined in the book of Liping Ma (1999, 2010) on "profound understanding of fundamental mathematics (PUFM)". Ball and her colleagues call the kind of content understanding described by Schoenfeld and Kilpatrick, "mathematical content knowledge for teaching" (Ball et al. 2005, 2008). In her earlier work, Ball (1990) proposed four dimensions of subject matter knowledge for teaching that mathematics teachers need to have. These dimensions include: (1) possessing correct knowledge of concepts and procedures; (2) understanding the underlying principles and meanings; (3) knowing the connections among mathematical ideas, and (4) understanding the nature of mathematical knowledge and mathematics as a field (e.g., being able to determine what counts as an "answer" in mathematics? What establishes the validity of an answer? etc.).

In the work that followed, Ball and her colleagues (Ball et al. 2005) defined "mathematical content knowledge for teaching" as being composed of two key elements: "common" knowledge of mathematics that any well-educated adult should have and mathematical knowledge that is "specialized" to the work of teaching and that only teachers need know (p. 22). From their descriptions, it seems that "common" mathematical knowledge is equivalent to being able to do mathematics, whereas "specialized" mathematical knowledge consists of being able to do mathematics and to know why (i.e., the reasoning that teachers need to know in order to teach students).

The notion that there is content knowledge unique to teaching was further expanded in their most recent work. Ball and her colleagues (Ball et al. 2008) proposed a sub-domain of "pure" content knowledge unique to the work of teaching, which they call *specialized content knowledge* (italics emphasized by the authors). The distinction between *specialized content knowledge* and other knowledge of mathematics, according to these authors, is that the former is needed by teachers for specific tasks of teaching (e.g., responding to students' why questions) and is not intertwined with knowledge of pedagogy, students, curriculum, or other non-content domains. This *specialized content knowledge* in principle seems similar to Liping Ma's (1999, 2010) proposed concept of "profound understanding of fundamental mathematics" (PUFM).

Ma proposed the concept of PUFM in her much celebrated work on teachers' understanding of four standard topics in elementary school mathematics between a group of Chinese and American teachers. According to Ma (1999), a teacher with PUFM is one who:

> ...is aware of the "simple but powerful" basic ideas of mathematics and tends to revisit and reinforce them. He or she has a fundamental understanding of the whole elementary mathematics curriculum, thus is ready to exploit an opportunity to review concepts that students have previously studied or to lay the groundwork for a concept to be studied later. (p. 124)

Ma specified four properties of understanding that characterize PUFM, namely, basic ideas, connectedness, multiple representations, and longitudinal coherence. Shulman (1999) calls these four properties of understanding "a powerful framework for grasping the mathematical content necessary to understand and instruct the thinking of schoolchildren" (p. xi).

In summary, several characteristics of content understanding central to teaching are commonly emphasised in the seminar work by leading education researchers and mathematicians. These characteristics tend to cluster around coherence (e.g., connectedness among mathematical concepts), reasoning (e.g., using definitions as a basis for logical reasoning), and purposefulness and/or key ideas (e.g., being mindful of why one is to study a concept and how the concept might be related to prior or later topics). These central characteristics are the basis of our framework for conceptual understanding of mathematical topics.

OUR FRAMEWORK OF MATHEMATICAL CONTENT UNDERSTANDING

Our framework of mathematical content understanding is centrally concerned with delineating characteristics of knowledge that demonstrate a relational understanding of a mathematical topic (i.e., knowing what to do and why) (Wu 2011c), as opposed to an instrumental understanding which Skemp (1976/2006) regarded as knowing the "rules without reasons." In other words, from a relational understanding perspective, to say one knows or understands a mathematical idea implies one knows:

what it says precisely,
what it says intuitively,
why it is true,
why it is worth knowing,
in what way it can be put to use, [and]
the natural context in which it appears. Wu (2011c)

Integrating the emphasis of reasoning and understanding, the key ideas proposed by education researchers (e.g., Ball et al. 2008; Ma 1999, 2010; Schoenfeld and Kilpatrick 2008), and Wu's five characteristics of mathematics (Wu 2010, 2011a, b), we define three characteristics that exemplify mathematical content understanding. Table 6.1 lists these three characteristics, what each characteristic means, and prior scholars' work that contributed to our conception of each characteristic.

The following sections describe what conceptual understanding of foundational mathematical topics look like using the framework as a guide. These foundational topics include place value, number line, and the connection between whole number and fraction operations, fraction division (why invert and multiply), linear equation and graph (constant speed, slope, different forms of linear equations), and quadratic function and graph (different forms of quadratic functions, quadratic formula, and root(s) of a quadratic function assuming the discriminant is greater than or equal to zero). The central questions guiding conceptual understanding of these topics include:

1. Where did the concept of place value come from and why is the concept central to whole number operations?
2. What is number line? Why does number line play a central role in connecting whole numbers, fractions, and their mathematical operations? In other words, why does number line play an important role in helping students transfer their learning and understanding of whole numbers and operations to the learning of fractions?
3. What does fraction division mean and why invert and multiply when dividing fractions?
4. What is the assumption underlying proportionality in mathematics problems?
5. Why can the slope of a line be calculated using any two distinctive points on the line? How does knowing this fact free students from mechanic memorizations of different forms of linear equations?
6. What is the connection among different forms of linear equations?
7. What is the graph of quadratic function? Why understanding the graph of quadratic function would set students on the path to understand the relationships among different forms of quadratic functions? In other words, why do we even need different forms of quadratic functions? How does quadratic formula fit in all of this? What do we know about the connection between the roots of a quadratic function (assuming the discriminant is greater than or equal to zero) and the constants (a, b, c) in a quadratic function?

Conceptual understanding of mathematical topics means to be able to answer these questions with precision, coherence, and purposefulness (i.e., the three characteristics outlined in Table 6.1).

PLACE VALUE

The concept of place value plays a central role in whole number arithmetic and is one of the key mathematical topics taught to elementary students at a young age. The typical way the concept is introduced to students, however, does not emphasize where the concept came from (i.e., its mathematical meaning) or why the concept is important (e.g., the fact that place value is behind all whole number operations). As shown in Chap. 2 of this book, when students are first exposed to the concept of place value, they see examples of numbers (e.g., a two-digit number). The teacher would then tell them that each "number" (note: digit would be more accurate) occupies a different *place*, such as the ones place or tens place and that is what we mean by place value. They are also told the fact that 1 ten makes 10 ones and 10 ones make up 1 ten. This is not to say that the teacher is at fault, because this is the way he or she was taught and this is what is prescribed in the math textbook used to teach the concept.

In contrast to the rote teaching and learning of the concept, students should have opportunities to learn where the concept came from, which requires making explicit the connection between how we count whole numbers in our numeral system and the concept of place value. This connection (i.e., counting, place value, and the expanded form of a whole number) will also help students see how the concept is at work for whole number operations. The concept of place value plays a central role in the Hindu-Arabic numeral system (i.e., the decimal numeral system), because place value allows us to represent all possible counting numbers by using only 10 symbols, namely, 0, 1, 2, 3, 4, 5, 6, 7, 8 and 9 (for a detailed exposition of this topic, see Sections 1.1 and 1.2 of Wu 2011b).

Take a look at this number: 1,383,896,747. This number represents the population of China as of 9:45 a.m. Eastern Daylight Saving Time (of the USA) on September 29, 2016. This is a very large number. Note there are two 3's occupying two different places in this number, the 7th and the 9th place respectively (reading from right to left). The 3 in the 7th place stands for 3 million, whereas 3 in the 9th place stands for 3 hundred million. Where did these two meanings for 3 come from? Wu (2011b) gave a good counting example to illustrate the origin of place value. Suppose we are counting and are allowed to have only one place (but with all 10 symbols). The best we can do is:

$$0,1,2,3,4,5,6,7,8,9$$

Since we are allowed to have only one place, after exhausting the first row (i.e., 0 to 9), the best we can do is to repeat the procedure:

$$0,1,2,3,4,5,6,7,8,9$$

And keep going until infinity.

The problem with having only one place is that we are unable to distinguish 3 in the first row (i.e., counting three steps from 0 in the first row) from 3 in the second row (counting 13 steps from 0 in the first row). But this problem can be avoided if we allow ourselves to have more than one place. This breakthrough (i.e., allowing our counting system to have more than one place) is where the concept of place value came from. For example, we need 10 places when counting the population of China (i.e., 1,383,896,747), namely, ones, tens, a hundred, a thousand, ten thousand, a hundred thousand, a million, ten million, a hundred million, and a billion.

Having students see the connection between the concept of place value and the decimal numeral counting system could enlighten them to see the relationship between different places (so to speak). For instance, when we go from the ones place to tens place, the rate is 10. Similarly, when we go from the tens place to the hundred place, the rate is 10 also because of the way counting works in the decimal system. Therefore, the digit 3 in the two-digit number 33 means two different things. The 3 in the ones place means 3 ones or 3, whereas the 3 in the tens place means 3 tens, or 30. And an alternative way to represent 33 would be $3 \times 10 + 3 \times 1$ (i.e., the expanded form of the two-digit number 33). In a similar manner, the digit 3 in the three-digit number 333 means three different things, 3 hundred, 3 tens, and 3 ones ($3 \times 100 + 3 \times 10 + 3 \times 1$).

To summarize, a conceptual understanding of the concept of place value means that students should have opportunities to learn where the concept came from, why the concept is central, and how the concept underlies all whole number operations. This point became evident and is validated as we look back at classroom mathematics teaching and learning (see Chap. 2).

NUMBER LINE, WHOLE NUMBERS, FRACTIONS, AND OPERATIONS

Americans' phobia of fractions is a well-known fact. This phenomenon is understandable when one thinks about how fractions are taught to students. Instead of helping students learn the connection between whole numbers and fractions, fractions are taught as a completely different number system from whole numbers. Instead of helping students see the intrinsically similar logic between whole number operations and fraction operations, fraction operations are taught completely disconnected from whole number operations. To have a conceptual understanding of fractions and their operations, we need to help students learn the connection between the two (i.e., whole numbers and fractions) and help them realize the fact that what they learn about whole number operations transfers 100 percent to fractions. In order to do this, however, we will first need to define for them what a number or fraction is by utilizing the number line. The seminal work on the mathematical development of fractions in the past two decades that makes use of the number line was initiated in 1998 by Wu (see "Teaching fractions in elementary school: A manual for teachers," accessible at https://math.berkeley.edu/~wu/fractions1998.pdf) and the outline was completed in 2002 (see "Chapter 2: Fractions (Draft)," accessible at https://math.berkeley.edu/~wu/EMI2a.pdf). Wu's seminal work on fractions utilizing the number line was incorporated in the Mathematics Common Core Standards' approach to teaching fractions.

So if we utilize the following number line (draw a line, choose a point of origin, 0, and define a unit segment):

$$0---1---2---3---4---5---6---7---8---9$$

With this number line, we define a whole number 7 as counting 7 unit segments from the origin 0. In a similar manner, fraction $\frac{2}{3}$, would be to count 2 unit segments $\frac{1}{3}$ from the origin 0, with the unit segment $\frac{1}{3}$ defined as dividing 1 into three equal parts and each part is $\frac{1}{3}$. So just like a whole number, a fraction is also a number. To illustrate these central ideas, let us take a look at two topics involving fractions, namely, what dividing fractions means and why we invert and multiply when we divide fractions. Table 6.2 lists scenario questions that are used to investigate a group of undergraduate STEM majors' understanding of fraction division and foundational algebra topics. Scenarios 1.1 to 1.3 focused on the topics of fraction division and why invert and multiple when dividing fractions. The emphasis is that a conceptual understanding of these topics means helping students see the connection between whole number division and fraction division. This understanding is characterized by precision, coherence, and purposefulness. In a similar vein, scenarios 2.1 to 2.4 focused on linear equation and graph, while scenarios 3.1 to 3.2 focused on quadratic function and graph. These scenarios intended to get at questions 4 to 7 listed earlier. The ability to answer these questions with precision, coherence, and purposefulness is an indication of what it means to have a

Table 6.2   Focus and key mathematical ideas underlying the scenario questions for each topic

Math topic	Question focus	Scenario questions	Key mathematics ideas
Dividing fractions	1.1: What does dividing fractions mean?	Imagine that you are teaching a group of *6th graders* to solve the following problem:[a]	Definitions of: whole numbers, fractions Definitions of: dividing whole numbers, dividing fractions
		A rope $43\frac{3}{8}$ meters long is cut into pieces which are each $\frac{5}{3}$ meters long.	
		How many such pieces can we get out of the rope? 1.1 Describe how you would approach this problem with your students in a way that builds on their prior mathematical knowledge and/or skills related to division of whole numbers	
		1.2 Suppose your answer is $A\frac{B}{C}$ where A, B, and C are whole numbers so that $0 < B < C$. How would you explain to students what the A means and what the $\frac{B}{C}$ means?	
	1.2: see 1.1	See above	Division as an alternative, but equivalent way of writing multiplication Distributive law Definition of mixed number Representation using number line
	1.3: Why invert and multiply when dividing fractions?	1.3 Imagine that one of your *6th graders* missed your lesson on fraction division. He studies the textbook and attempts the homework on his own. The next day he comes and tells you,	**Definition of dividing fractions→why invert and multiply?**
		"The book says $\frac{17}{8} \div \frac{5}{9} = \frac{17}{8} \times \frac{9}{5}$, but I don't understand why." How would you respond to this student?	

Linear equation and graph	2.1: What is the assumption or key mathematical concept underlying so-called proportional reasoning?	2.1 You are giving your *7th graders* the district pre-algebra common assessment. One word problem on the assessment reads as follows: "Abe is training for the Boston marathon, so he runs every day. This morning he ran 4 miles in 40 minutes. How many miles did he run in the first 20 minutes? Show your work." One of your top-performing students in the class, nicknamed "Einstein," comes to you with her test and says, "There is not enough information given to solve this problem." 1. How would you respond to "Einstein"? 2. Explain how you would teach the class about the critical mathematical concept(s) for solving this kind of word problem	Assumption: definition of constant rate→implications for solving so-called proportional problems Definition of division Linear function without constant term (for higher grades)
	2.2: See 2.1.	2.2 You are teaching a class of *8th graders* and writing a test to assess their ability to translate word problems into symbolic equations. Come up with a story that could be represented by the equation: $y = \dfrac{7}{5}x + 4$	Assumption: constant rate or speed
	2.3: why the slope of a line can be calculated using *any* two distinctive points on the line?	2.3 How would you help *8th graders* understand that the slope of a non-vertical line can be calculated using any two distinct points on the line (e.g., the slope of the line below can be calculated with points P_1 and P_2 or points P_3 and P_4)? 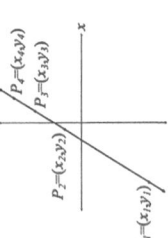	Definition: slope of a line Independence of any two distinct points when calculating the slope Similar triangles based on the angle-angle criterion
	2.4: What is the connection among different forms of linear equation?	2.4 Suppose you are teaching a class of *9th graders* about graphs of linear equations in two variables. Explain how you would help students see the connection among: the standard form $ax + by = c$ where a, b, c are constants and $a \neq 0$ or $b \neq 0$ the slope-intercept form $y = mx + k$ where m, k are constants the point-slope form $y - q = m(x - p)$ where p, q are constants the graph of a linear equation	Connection between linear equation in two variables and its graph: (1) definition of the graph—collection of all ordered pairs (x_0, y_0) that satisfy equation, $ax + by = c$; (2) the graph of a linear equation is a straight line; every straight line is the graph of some linear equation; (3) the slope of a line can be calculated using any two distinct points on the line. (Note: facts (2) and (3) can be proved)

(continued)

Table 6.2 (continued)

| Quadratic functions and graphs | 3.1: the graph of quadratic function | 3.1 You and your colleagues are discussing struggles your *10th graders* have in learning quadratic functions. As a group, you are trying to figure out how best to help students overcome the struggles. You decide that one approach is to help students "see" the connection between a quadratic function and its graph.

Let g and f be the quadratic functions $g(x) = x^2$ and $f(x) = ax^2 + bx + c$ where a, b, and c are constants and $a \neq 0$. Describe how you would use the graph of g to help students see how one arrives at the graph of f | Definition of graph of a quadratic function
Graphs of all quadratic functions are similar to the graph of the unit quadratic function $g(x) = x^2$; and graphs of all quadratic functions are congruent to the graph of some standard quadratic function of the form $f_s(x) = ax^2$ through translation (a fact that can be proved) |
| | 3.2: different forms of quadratic function | 3.2 How would you help students understand that $f(x) = ax^2 + bx + c$ can be rewritten into the forms $a(x-h)^2 + k$ and $a(x-p)(x-q)$ where h, k, p, and q are suitable constants and assuming the discriminant $b^2 - 4ac \geq 0$? How would you explain the relationship among the constants a, b, c, h, k, p, and q? | Completing the square and why it's central for learning quadratic functions
Definitions of: root of quadratic equation, zero of quadratic function
Relationship between roots and constants in each form of the quadratic function |

conceptual understanding of key concepts and topics involving linear equation and quadratic function. To reiterate, this exposition of mathematical conceptual understanding has just begun to receive attention and was by no means commonplace or available in the mathematics or mathematics education literature until now.

What does dividing fractions mean? We used scenario questions 1.1 and 1.2 (see Table 6.2) to get at participants' understanding.

An exemplary response to these questions clearly exhibits characteristics of precision, coherence, and purposefulness. Consider the following response. Note that the response shows a deliberate effort at invoking students' prior mathematical knowledge and familiarity with whole numbers:

> *In order to build on students' prior knowledge of whole numbers, we assume that students have been exposed to the definition of a whole number as a point on the number line. This way of defining whole numbers will put whole numbers and fractions on the same footing in the real number system, which will make the subsequent teaching of dividing fractions a little easier if students are helped to see the parallel logic of dividing whole numbers and that of dividing fractions. So before I teach students how to set up the problem and solve it, I would first ask questions such as: What is a whole number? Can you give me some examples of whole numbers? What about some examples where whole numbers are used to describe quantities of things? Etc.*

Here, the response shows a deliberate effort at scaffolding mathematical ideas by emphasizing the need to help students see the connection between how whole numbers and fractions are defined. In addition, the response is very purposeful and clear about what numbers and fractions are and seeing the "parallel logic" between the two. The purposefulness and clarity paves the way for easier grasping of a new topic (i.e., dividing fractions) based on prior knowledge (i.e., dividing whole numbers). As the response continues:

> *After this initial questioning and answering exercise, I would pose the following problem to students: A rope of 44 meters long is cut into pieces which are each 2 meters long. How many such pieces can we get out of the rope? Sixth graders probably are well trained enough to immediately figure out what they need to do (i.e., $44 \div 2 = 22$). After they have done the division and get an answer, I would ask them to explain why they divide? What does the definition of division of whole numbers mean? How can we represent this on the number line? Etc. The key mathematical ideas I hope to reach common understanding*

among students are: (1) Dividing two whole numbers A ÷ B means that there is a unique whole number C that makes C × B = A true. In this context, it means 22 × 4 = 44, or 44 = 22 × 2; (2) Division is an alternative way of writing multiplication (i.e., A ÷ B = C is an alternative way of writing C × B = A); and (3) Using the number line to graphically represent what dividing 44 ÷ 2 means (i.e., if we cut the rope of 44 meters into pieces that are 2 meters each, 22 is the 22nd point on the number line when counting by 2 meters and coincides with the 44-meter point).

Note here again the response is deliberate at connecting what students knew (i.e., dividing whole numbers) with what they are about to learn (i.e., dividing fractions). Furthermore, the response uses definition as a basis for logical reasoning (*what does dividing fractions mean?*) behind why we divide. In addition, the response demonstrates an understanding of the interconnectedness of mathematical ideas. In this case, the response emphasizes the algebraic (44 ÷ 2) and the geometric representations of dividing whole numbers using the number line. Finally, note how the response emphasizes the key mathematical ideas that students should be able to walk away with. With this solid foundation, students are ready to set up the problem as one that involves dividing fractions, as shown below:

Building on these key mathematical ideas related to whole numbers, I would then point out to students that, since fractions are points on a number line, what we can do with whole numbers, we can do the same with fractions. Hopefully students then will be able to set up the problem as: $43\frac{3}{8} \div \frac{5}{3} = ?$ *At this point, students have to be taught at least how to divide fractions (i.e., at least the mechanics of dividing fractions have to be taught prior to the lesson of solving this problem) so that they can carry out the calculation, which gives* $26\frac{1}{40}$ *. Of course, students should be helped to understand why they invert and multiply (this part will be picked up in scenario 1B).*

Here again the response emphasizes a key idea (i.e., *since fractions are points on a number line, what we can do with whole numbers, we can do the same with fractions*). This emphasis helps students to see the interconnectedness between dividing whole numbers and dividing fractions. Furthermore, the response is deliberate at scaffolding these ideas by invoking students' prior mathematical knowledge. So what does dividing fractions mean?

So how do we interpret what we got in this particular problem's context? Two key ideas underlie this question: (1) first is to remind students that division is an alternative way of writing multiplication, and (2) the distributive law. Therefore, I would ask student what would be an alternative way to write:

$$43\frac{3}{8} \div \frac{5}{3} = 26\frac{1}{40}.$$

Building on what we talked about using the whole numbers (i.e., a 44-meter long rope cut into pieces 2 meters long each), students probably will be able to write down:

$$43\frac{3}{8} = 26\frac{1}{40} \times \frac{5}{3}$$

$$= \left(26 + \frac{1}{40}\right) \times \frac{5}{3} \leftarrow \text{definition of mixed number}$$

$$\left(\text{a sum of a whole number and a proper fraction}\right)$$

$$= 26 \times \frac{5}{3} + \frac{1}{40} \times \frac{5}{3} \leftarrow \text{distributive}$$

So the expanded expression means that, when we cut the rope into pieces that are $\frac{5}{3}$ meters each, we get 26 pieces of $\frac{5}{3}$ meters segment, plus a fraction of a $\frac{5}{3}$ meters segment (i.e., $\frac{1}{40}$ of $\frac{5}{3}$).

Here again the response is purposeful about emphasizing key mathematical ideas (*Two key ideas underlie this question*) and about scaffolding from simple to complex (i.e., *Building on what we talked about using the whole numbers, i.e., 44 meters long rope cut into pieces 2 meters long each*). In addition, the response is keen on using the definition (i.e., division as a different but equivalent way of writing multiplication) as the basis for logical reasoning that leads to an understanding of what dividing fractions means. Furthermore, the response emphasizes that students see how dividing fractions can be represented on the number line:

What does this look like on the number line? I would have students draw the number line and set out the total length of $43\frac{3}{8}$ meters. Then from the origin *(i.e., 0), taking segments of $\frac{5}{3}$ meters, we would get 26 whole pieces or segments*

of $\frac{5}{3}$ meters. In other words, the 26th point is the number $26 \times \frac{5}{3}$. The fraction

part, $\frac{1}{40}$ of $\frac{5}{3}$ means we divide the next $\frac{5}{3}$ segment into 40 equal parts, and

the 1st point (as we count from the left endpoint of this $\frac{5}{3}$ segment) is the frac-

tion part $\frac{1}{40}$ of $\frac{5}{3}$ and has length $\frac{5}{40 \times 3} = \frac{5}{120}$. This final point represents the

number $26 \times \frac{5}{3} + \frac{1}{40} \times \frac{5}{3}$, which coincides with the point $43\frac{3}{8}$ on the number

line.

Here again the response demonstrates the interconnectedness of mathematical ideas by emphasizing the multiple representations (i.e., algebraic and geometric) of what dividing fractions mean.

In summary, this exemplary response consistently emphasizes the key mathematical idea, its rationale, the logical progression of mathematical concepts, and the connectedness among different mathematical concepts, procedures, and ideas. In addition, the response shows attention to how to scaffold mathematical ideas to students (e.g., from simple to complex; from specific to general). Overall, the response exemplifies precision, coherence, and purposefulness, the key principles that characterize content understanding for teaching.

Why invert and multiply when dividing fractions? Though most students know the invert and multiply rule when dividing fractions, few understand why invert and multiply works. We used scenario question 1.3 (see Table 6.2) to get at participants' understanding of the invert and multiple rule when dividing fractions.

An exemplary response to this scenario question begins with an explicit definition of what dividing fractions means, as shown below:

First, I would help the student review what $\dfrac{17}{8} \div \dfrac{5}{9}$ means—i.e., what does it mean to divide fractions? Using the number line again, set out $\dfrac{17}{8}$; how many $\dfrac{5}{9}$ do we get? What is another way of writing this division problem? By the definition of dividing fractions, $\dfrac{17}{8} \div \dfrac{5}{9}$ is the unique fraction C that satisfies $\dfrac{17}{8} = C \times \dfrac{5}{9}$.

With the meaning of dividing fractions defined, the response proceeds to the logical next step, that is, what is this unique fraction?

So how do we know what this unique fraction is in this context? First, let us find one fraction that satisfies this equation. Since $\dfrac{9}{5} \times \dfrac{5}{9} = 1$ then $\dfrac{17}{8} = \dfrac{17}{8} \times 1 = \dfrac{17}{8} \times \dfrac{9}{5} \times \dfrac{5}{9}$. Can I rewrite the above equation as: $\dfrac{17}{8} = \left(\dfrac{17}{8} \times \dfrac{9}{5}\right) \times \dfrac{5}{9}$? Yes, because of the associative law of multiplication. Now, look at this new equation. What does it remind you? Compare it to the definition of division, i.e., $\dfrac{17}{8} \div \dfrac{5}{9}$ is the unique fraction C that satisfies $\dfrac{17}{8} = C \times \dfrac{5}{9}$, we can see that $\dfrac{17}{8} \times \dfrac{9}{5}$ is such a C. This response then connects the definition with $\left(\dfrac{17}{8} \times \dfrac{9}{5}\right)$ as a possible answer to the division of $\dfrac{17}{8} \div \dfrac{5}{9}$.

Now, how do we know $\left(\dfrac{17}{8} \times \dfrac{9}{5}\right)$ is the unique solution? Is it possible that a different solution (i.e., fraction) exists out there? So if C is any solution to $\dfrac{17}{8} = C \times \dfrac{5}{9}$, how do we know that this C must be equal to $\left(\dfrac{17}{8} \times \dfrac{9}{5}\right)$? Let us see. If $\dfrac{17}{8} = C \times \dfrac{5}{9}$, by multiplying both sides with $\dfrac{9}{5}$, we get $\dfrac{17}{8} \times \dfrac{9}{5} = \left(C \times \dfrac{5}{9}\right) \times \dfrac{9}{5} = C \times \left(\dfrac{5}{9} \times \dfrac{9}{5}\right) = C \times 1 = C$. Therefore $\left(\dfrac{17}{8} \times \dfrac{9}{5}\right)$ is the only (unique) fraction that solves the equation.

So by definition $\left(\dfrac{17}{8} \times \dfrac{9}{5}\right)$ *is the unique fraction or solution to this division*

problem $\dfrac{17}{8} \div \dfrac{5}{9}$, *which is where "invert and multiply" comes from.*

In addition to using explicit definitions as the basis for logical reasoning, an exemplary response also exhibits coherence in terms of being deliberate at scaffolding mathematical ideas from simple to complex and specific to general, as shown below:

After working through this specific problem with the student, I would also help him see the general principle (i.e., "invert and multiply" works for dividing all fractions) using symbols. Let $\dfrac{m}{n}$ and $\dfrac{k}{l}$ be fractions where m, n, k, l are whole numbers and n, k, l are non-zero. Then the goal is to prove $\dfrac{m}{n} \div \dfrac{k}{l} = \dfrac{ml}{nk}$. The key is to enable the student to see that the reason why the particular division problem above (i.e., concrete numbers in the scenario) works is exactly the same when the specific numbers are replaced with symbols that stand for whole numbers.

Note the response is purposeful about what they are doing, emphasizing the goal of the mathematical activity (*the goal is to prove* $\dfrac{m}{n} \div \dfrac{k}{l} = \dfrac{ml}{nk}$) and the key idea (*The key is to enable the student to see that the reason why the particular division problem above (i.e., concrete numbers in the scenario) works is exactly the same when the specific numbers are replaced with symbols that stand for whole numbers*). Apart from purposefulness, the response here is also helping students make a connection between something unfamiliar (i.e., using symbols) with something familiar (i.e., using concrete fractions). By emphasizing coherence, the response helps students see the interconnectedness of mathematical ideas.

As before, we will first show that there is one fraction that satisfies $\dfrac{m}{n} = C * \left(\dfrac{k}{l}\right)$,

*and then show that **any** other solution C has to be equal to $\dfrac{m}{n} \times \dfrac{l}{k}$ or $\dfrac{ml}{nk}$.*

First, let us find one fraction that satisfies this equation.

Just as $\dfrac{9}{5} \times \dfrac{5}{9} = 1$, we have $\dfrac{l}{k} \times \dfrac{k}{l} = 1$. Therefore:

$$\frac{m}{n} = \frac{m}{n} \times 1$$

$$= \frac{m}{n} \times \frac{l}{k} \times \frac{k}{l}$$

$$= \left(\frac{m}{n} \times \frac{l}{k}\right) \times \frac{l}{k} \leftarrow \text{product rule for fraction multiplication}$$

$$= \left(\frac{ml}{nk}\right) \times \frac{k}{l} \leftarrow \text{associative law of multiplication}$$

So what is $\frac{m}{n} = \left(\frac{ml}{nk}\right) \times \frac{k}{l}$? *This is the multiplication representation of dividing the two fractions* $\frac{m}{n}$ *and* $\frac{k}{l}$; *or put it in a different way, it's the definition of dividing fractions:* $\frac{m}{n} \div \frac{k}{l}$ *is defined as* $\frac{m}{n} = (C) \times \frac{k}{l}$ *so because* $\frac{m}{n} = \left(\frac{ml}{nk}\right) \times \frac{k}{l}$, *we conclude* $\frac{ml}{nk}$ *is such a C.*

Now, how do we know $\frac{ml}{nk}$ *is the unique solution? Is it possible that a different solution (i.e., fraction) exists out there? So if C is any solution to* $\frac{m}{n} = C \times \frac{k}{l}$, *how do we know that this C must be equal to* $\frac{ml}{nk}$? *Let us see. If* $\frac{m}{n} = C \times \frac{k}{l}$, *by multiplying both sides with* $\frac{l}{k}$, *we get* $\frac{m}{n} \times \frac{l}{k} = \left(C \times \frac{k}{l}\right) \times \frac{l}{k} = C \times \left(\frac{k}{l} \times \frac{l}{k}\right) = C \times 1 = C.$ *Therefore* $\left(\frac{m}{n} \times \frac{l}{k}\right)$ *is the only (unique) fraction that solves the equation.*

So by definition $\left(\frac{m}{n} \times \frac{l}{k}\right)$ *is the unique fraction or solution to this division problem* $\left(\frac{m}{n} \div \frac{k}{l}\right)$, *which is where "invert and multiply" comes from.*

Again in this example, we see how the responses exemplify precision, coherence, and purposefulness, the key principles that characterize content understanding for teaching.

PROPORTIONALITY, SLOPE, LINEAR EQUATION, AND ITS GRAPH

What is the assumption or key mathematical concept underlying proportionality mathematics problems? Proportionality occupies a significant role in algebra because it is used to teach students how to solve word problems dealing with speed, rate, and so on. One important amiss, however, lies in the fact that students are never taught about the key mathematical idea underlying such problems, i.e., making explicit the assumption we make in order to solve proportionality mathematics problems. Scenario questions 2.1 and 2.2 (see Table 6.2) are used to probe participants' awareness of this issue. Since question 2.2 asks respondents to come up with a story, an exemplary response is one that is explicit about the underlying assumption needed to solve the problem. The discussion here focuses on question 2.1. Below is an exemplary response to this question:

The people who wrote this problem made an assumption. Can you see what it was? They assumed that Abe runs at a constant speed. Does that help you solve the problem?

"Einstein" might only need this much information. But she might need more, in which case the teacher might continue as follows:

So what does running at a constant speed mean? First, I would ask students how we calculate the average speed for Abe, which is:
Average speed run during any time interval from t_1 to t_2 =

$$\frac{\text{distance traveled from } t_1 \text{ to } t_2}{t_1 - t_2}$$

To say that Abe is running at a constant speed, by definition, means that the average speed for any time interval is a constant (or fixed) number, which we'll call "v".

Note the respondent immediately focuses on the key idea (i.e., *the key to solving this problem is to assume that Abe runs at a constant speed*).

Then the respondent continues the line of reasoning by asking for the meaning of "running at a constant speed." To do this, the respondent invokes a related idea, i.e., average speed, because this concept is the basis for defining constant speed (i.e., *"To say that Abe is running at a constant speed, by definition, means that the average speed for any time interval is a constant (or fixed) number"*). Here the respondent is very deliberate about using the definition as a basis for helping students "see" what reasoning makes it possible to set up proportionality problems, as shown below:

Let D_1 be the distance traveled from time = 0 to t_1 and D_2 be the distance traveled from time = 0 to t_2. Then:

$$v = \frac{D_2 - D_1}{t_2 - t_1}$$

By the definition of division, this is equivalent to

$$D_2 - D_1 = v(t_2 - t_1)$$

Let t represent time (t > 0) and D represent the distance traveled from time = 0 to t. Then we can rewrite the above equation as:

$$\Delta D = v(\Delta t)$$

Furthermore, if we consider the time interval 0 to any time t, we get:

$$D = vt$$

This is a linear equation in two variables, t and D, without the constant term. It's important to see that the key idea used to arrive at this equation is the definition of constant speed.

Building on the definition of constant speed, the respondent uses definition again (i.e., definition of division) to rewrite the equation into a form that helps them to connect the definition of constant speed and linear equations in two variables without the constant term. This is the basis for the so-called proportionality reasoning that is used to solve a wide variety of problems involving speed, rate, etc.

Finally, the respondent is keenly aware of how what they are learning at the 8th grade might be connected with the mathematical concept they will learn later, i.e., function.

[Note: Later when students are introduced to the linear function, I'd also help them make the connection that the underlying mathematical concept for problems of constant speed or rate is a linear function in one variable without the constant term.]

Overall, the respondent is very purposeful in his or her reasoning and shows deliberate effort at using definition as a basis for logical reasoning and making explicit the interconnectedness of mathematical ideas at different levels of complexity.

Why can the slope of a line be calculated using *any* two distinct points on the line? Slope features prominently when teaching linear equations in the K-12 curriculum. Much of the emphasis in the textbook focuses more on the mechanical calculation than on the conceptual understanding of the concept of slope or the connection between linear equation and its graph. We used scenario question 2.3 to investigate respondents' understanding of the concept of slope and the connection between linear equation and its graph.

An exemplary response to this scenario question begins with the definition of the slope of a line:

The key mathematical idea underlying this question is that the slope of a line can be calculated using any two points on the line (i.e., independence of any two distinct points on the line). So how can we help students learn this key idea? Before I use P_1, P_2, P_3, P_4 as shown in the picture, I would first review with students how the slope of a line may be defined: given a line and assuming it slants upward (as the picture shows), let's take a point P on the line, go 1 unit horizontally to point R, then go upward (or vertically) and let the vertical line from R intersect the given line at point Q. Then the definition of slope is the length of segment QR (i.e., |QR|).

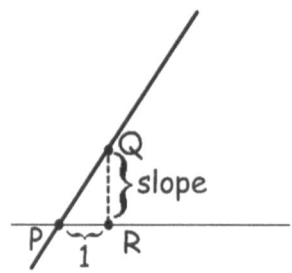

Here the respondent is laying a foundation for what comes next by precisely defining the slope of a line and showing this on the graph. Note how the respondent expands the definition and stretches students' thinking by posing the next question:

> *But how are we certain that this vertical length |QR| is the same for any point P we choose on the line? In other words: if we take another point P' on the line, go 1 unit horizontally to point R' and then go upward to intersect the line at point Q', how do we know that |QR| = |Q'R'|?*

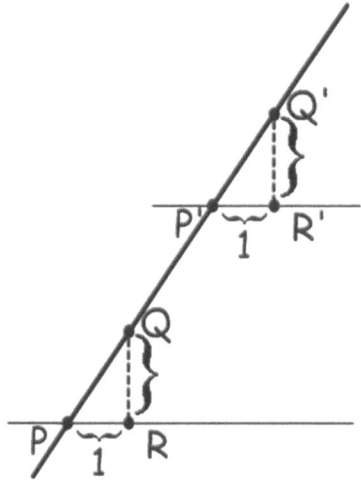

To answer this question, students need to invoke their knowledge of congruent triangles. This is an important step towards defining the slope precisely and completely, as the respondent points out:

> *I would expect the following explanation from students: |<PQR| = |<P'Q'R'|, |<QPR| = |<Q'P'R'| (corresponding angles on parallel lines) and |PR| = |P'R'| = 1, so by the angle-angle-side criterion, ΔPQR ≅ ΔP'Q'R' and, thus, |QR| = |Q'R'|. Therefore, the slope is independent of the point P and it makes sense to talk about the slope of the line.*

With the definition complete, the respondent adds complexity by posing the following question: *"Can we find another, more flexible way of finding the slope of a line, without having to measure 1 unit horizontally from a point on the line and then the vertical distance up?"* This step builds on the previous step of defining the slope of the line but uses similar triangles, as shown below:

> *To answer this question, let's do the following: let P, Q, R be as before (i.e., P is any point on the line used to define the slope of the line) and now suppose we take any other point on the line, call it S. From S, draw a vertical line and let it meet the horizontal line PR at point T.*

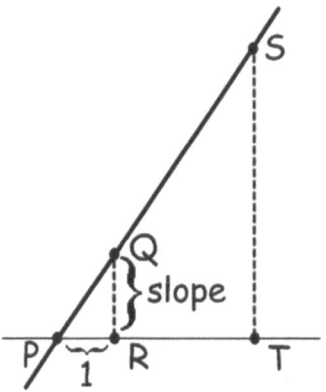

> *So now look at the two triangles, ΔPQR and ΔPST. What can we say about them? Hopefully students would recognize that they are similar triangles; if not, I'd tell them but ask them to prove (explain) why the triangles are similar (by the angle-angle criterion: right angles formed by perpendicular lines and correspond-ing angles on parallel lines).*
>
> *After establishing the fact that ΔPQR ~ ΔPST, I would then ask: what can we say about the relationship between the sides of the triangles? One of the things I would expect students to mention would be:*

$$\frac{|QR|}{|ST|} = \frac{|PR|}{|PT|}$$

> *Then I would guide them to manipulate the above equation into the following:*

$$\frac{|QR|}{|ST|} = \frac{|PR|}{|PT|} \Rightarrow |QR| = \frac{|PR| \cdot |ST|}{|PT|} \Rightarrow \frac{|QR|}{|PR|} = \frac{|ST|}{|PT|}$$

At this point, I would ask students what they observe. Hopefully they would recognize that, since $|PR| = 1$, the left side of the equation is equal to line segment $|QR|$, which is the slope of the line. In other words:

$$slope = \frac{|ST|}{|PT|}$$

Of course, the respondent is very purposeful about why they are doing this exercise:

From this exercise, I would hope students reached the following conclusions:

1. *The slope of the line can be calculated using points P (the point we used to define the slope) and S (any other point on the line).*
2. *We can calculate the slope of a line by dividing the length of the vertical line segment by the length of the horizontal line segment of $\triangle PST$.*

Because we had shown earlier that the point P used to define the slope is arbitrary (i.e., can be any point on the line) and we had defined S to be another arbitrary point on the line, then the conclusions above can be generalized into the following:

1. *The slope of the line can be calculated using any two distinct points, P and S, on the line.*
2. *We can calculate the slope of a line by dividing the length of the vertical line segment by the length of the horizontal line segment of $\triangle PST$ (or the negative of the ratio if the line slants to the left, i.e., \ ).*

This pedagogical scaffolding of a concept with key mathematical ideas in mind brings mathematical closure to students and we see how the respondent is very deliberate in scaffolding key ideas throughout the process. Having shown the underlying key ideas, the respondent then goes back to the original question (i.e., using P_1, P_2, P_3, and P_4) and has students work out the proof on their own:

To reinforce these main ideas, I would have students work in groups or pairs to prove (using similar triangle properties) that the slope of the line calculated by P_1, P_2 (in the original graph above) is the same as the slope calculated by P_3, P_4. Once they finish working in groups, I'd have a whole-class discussion and ask students to show how they did the proof. Below is an example of what I'd expect:

Draw in the horizontal and vertical lines through points P_1, P_2, P_3, P_4 and let them intersect at points Q and R as shown below:

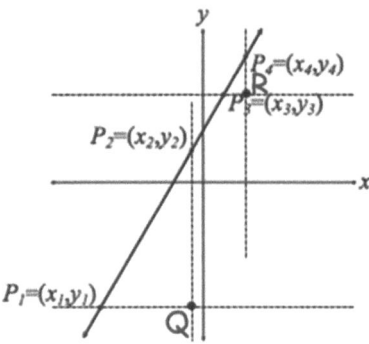

We claim that the two triangles formed, $\Delta P_1 P_2 Q$ and $\Delta P_3 P_4 R$, are similar. The reason is: $|\angle P_1 Q P_2| = |\angle P_3 R P_4|$ because both equal 90° and $|\angle P_1 P_2 Q| = |\angle P_3 P_4 R|$ because they are corresponding angles on parallel lines. Then, by the angle-angle criterion, $\Delta P_1 P_2 Q \sim \Delta P_3 P_4 R$. By the key triangle similarity theorem, we can then say $\dfrac{|P_2 Q|}{|P_4 R|} = \dfrac{|P_1 Q|}{|P_3 R|}$, and by multiplying both sides of the equation by $|P_4 R|$ and $\dfrac{1}{|P_1 Q|}$, we get $\dfrac{|P_2 Q|}{|P_1 Q|} = \dfrac{|P_4 R|}{|P_3 R|}$. That means the slope calculated by P_1, P_2 is the same as the slope calculated by P_3, P_4. Therefore, the slope can be calculated by any two distinct points on the line. And what is the length of the line segment for $P_2 Q$ and $P_1 Q$ respectively? From the graph, we see that it's $y_2 - y_1$ and $x_2 - x_1$. Similarly, we would get $y_4 - y_3$ and $x_4 - x_3$ for the length of the line segment for $P_4 R$ and $P_3 R$ respectively. What does all this tell us? It means that slope of the line could be represented as the ratio of $\dfrac{y_2 - y_1}{x_2 - x_1}$, or of $\dfrac{y_4 - y_3}{x_4 - x_3}$. This is where the popular phrase "rise over run" came about.

Looking at this exemplary response overall, we see that the respondent is mindful of the purpose of each activity, focuses on the key ideas and scaffolds these key ideas in a coherent way, starting with the definition, using it as a basis for subsequent logical reasoning, and leading students from simple ideas to more complex ones, from specific examples to general cases. In addition, the respondent explained where the popular formulaic definition of slope (i.e., "rise over run") came about.

What is the connection among different forms of linear equations?
A routine exercise that students in early algebra classes do is to memorize different forms of linear equations (e.g., standard form, point-slope form, two-point form, intercept-slope form, etc.). This rote learning deprives students of the opportunity to understand the connections among different forms of linear equations. For instance, students trained in rote learning are not given the opportunities to ponder the following questions: Why can a linear equation be written in different forms? What information is given in each form of the same linear equation? What is the connection among different forms? Can one go from one form to another? Knowing the answers to these questions will deepen students' understanding of linear equations. Scenario question 2.4 in Table 6.2 intends to probe study participants' understanding of these questions.

The exemplary response to the scenario question used to examine study participants' understanding of these questions is purposeful and focuses on the key mathematical ideas, as shown below:

> *The key idea is that students should not need to memorize different forms of linear equations (so that they mechanically match a particular given piece of information with a particular form). The key is to understand the connection between a linear equation in two variables and its graph, so that students can use any given information to figure out the equation of a line; or vice versa, given an equation, the students should know what its graph looks like.*

To help students understand these key ideas, the respondent again resorts to using definition as a basis for logical reasoning:

> *The following ideas are central to understanding the connection between a linear equation in two variables and its graph. So before addressing the question raised in the scenario, I'd want students to know the following facts:*
>
> – *Definition of the graph of a linear equation: collection of all ordered pairs (x_0, y_0) that satisfy the equation $ax + by = c$ (where $a \neq 0$ or $b \neq 0$).*
> – *The graph of a linear equation is a straight line; every straight line is the graph of some linear equation. [This is something that can be proved; though I might not do the proof with students right away, I'd at least point this out so that students know it can be proved.]*
> – *The slope of a line can be calculated using any two distinct points on the line.*

Having laid this foundation, the respondent begins a carefully orchestrated process of leading students to discover the key mathematical ideas:

With these basic understandings about a linear equation in two variables and its graph, I would first ask students to graph, by hand, the line 2x + 3y = 5. Then I'd ask them to work in groups or pairs to:

- *Calculate the slope and the y-intercept (i.e., when x=0).*
- *Show on the graph where/what is: slope and y-intercept.*

The purpose of this exercise is to get students to feel comfortable connecting algebraic calculations and graphical representations, especially as they relate to the slope and y-intercept.

Note the respondent begins with a concrete example and is very deliberate about the purpose behind this exercise: preparing students for what comes next:

Then I'd give students a line (say it's the graph of 3x – y = 2, just to make it easier), and ask them to figure out what the equation of the line is, if:

(1) We know one point and the slope.
(2) We know two points.
(3) We know the y-intercept and slope.

The specific steps may go something like this:

*(1) **Given slope and a point:***

> *Teacher prompt:*

Suppose the slope of a line is 3 and a point on the line is $P'(1,1)$ What's the equation of the line?

> *Expected student response:*

We've learned that the slope of a line can be calculated by using any two distinct points on the line. We know one point is given: $P'(1,1)$. Let $P(x,y)$ be any other point on the line. Then the slope is $\dfrac{y-1}{x-1}$. But we're also given that the slope is 3, so $\dfrac{y-1}{x-1} = 3$. By the definition of division, we get $y - 1 = 3(x - 1) \Rightarrow y - 1 = 3x - 3 \Rightarrow 3x - y = 2$.

[The interim step, $y - 1 = 3(x - 1)$, will be used later when I show them the generic point-slope form $y - q = m(x - p)$ and have students compare this step to the generic slope-intercept form.]

So far we've shown that every point on this line satisfies $3x - y = 2$. Is there any possibility that there are solutions (i.e., points) of $3x - y = 2$ that do not lie on this line? To address this issue, I would make sure that students know given a point P for instance, P $(1,1)$ and slope 3, there is one and only one line L passing through $(1,1)$ with the given slope 3.

(2) **Given two points:**

Teacher prompt:

Suppose a line contains points $P'(1,1)$ and $P''(0,-2)$. What's the equation of the line?

Expected student response:

Let $P(x, y)$ be any other point on the line besides $P'(1,1)$ or $P''(0,-2)$. Using the same reason as before (i.e., any two distinct points give the slope of the line), we get:

$$\frac{y-1}{x-1} = \frac{y-(-2)}{x-0} \Rightarrow \frac{y-1}{x-1} \Rightarrow xy - x = xy - y + 2x - 2 \Rightarrow 3x - y = 2$$

(3) **Given slope and y-intercept:**

Teacher prompt:

Suppose the slope of a line is 3 and the y-intercept of the line is -2. What's the equation of the line?
[Recall the earlier task where students used the graph to connect the y-intercept to the y-coordinate of the point where the line intersects the y-axis. The point of intersection is $(0, y_0)$ where y_0 is the y-intercept of the line.]

Expected student response:

We've learned that, because -2 is the y-intercept, then $(0, -2)$ is a point on the line. Let $P(x, y)$ be any other point on the line besides $(0, -2)$. Using the same reason as before (i.e., any two distinct points give the slope of the line), we get:

$$3 = \frac{y-(-2)}{x-0} \Rightarrow 3x = y + 2 \Rightarrow 3x - y = 2$$

[The alternative interim step, $3x - 2 = y$, will later be used to compare with the generic slope-intercept form, $y = mx + k$.]

The purpose of this exercise is to get students used to figuring out the equation when different pieces of information are given. I would forbid them to use the forms as given in the textbook; instead, I would ask students to figure out the equations based on their understandings of the definition of the graph of linear equation and the connection between linear equations and their graphs (listed at the start of this response).

Throughout these exercises, the respondent connects ideas that students have learned in the previous steps with what they are doing now. In addition, the respondent is purposeful about emphasizing key mathematical ideas and using definition as a basis for logical reasoning. The process of discovery is coherent, going from simple to complex and from specific to general:

Once students figured out the linear equations based on different pieces of given information, I'd ask them to arrange their equations in the forms as shown in the scenario questions (now I'd show them the forms which are popular in textbooks), compare their equations with the general cases (i.e., the symbols) and see what they think. For example, to get $3x - y = 2$ into the form $y = mx + b$, students would add y and subtract 2 from both sides of the equation.

I would then talk about the significance of the constants in the forms $y - q = m(x - p)$ and $y = mx + b$. Students should easily recognize the first form from case (1) above: given a line with slope m and point (p, q) and letting (x, y) be any other point on the line, we get: $m = \dfrac{y - q}{x - p} \Rightarrow y - q = m(x - p)$. So, that's why this form is called the point-slope form.

When we consider the form $y = mx + b$, students should easily see that the b is the y-intercept because $y = b$ when $x = 0$. However, what is the constant m? (Note: we don't know that the m in this form represents the same number m in the point-slope form above.) To answer this question, we do the following:

Say the equation of a line is: $y = mx + b$ where m and b are constants. Let $P_1(x_1, y_1)$ and $P_2(x_2, y_2)$ be two distinct points on the line. Because the two points are on the line, by definition, $y_1 = mx_1 + b$ and $y_2 = mx_2 + b$. Then what is the slope of the line?

$$slope = \frac{y_2 - y_1}{x_2 - x_1} = \frac{mx_2 + b - (mx_1 + b)}{x_2 - x_1} = \frac{mx_2 - mx_1}{x_2 - x_1} = \frac{m(x_2 - x_1)}{x_2 - x_1} = m$$

Note that the final step is possible because $x_1 \neq x_2$. Therefore, the m is the slope of the line, and that's why $y = mx + b$ is called the slope-intercept form.

Other things I'd look for in their understanding at this point:

- *The standard form is the most general form. It includes cases when b = 0 (i.e., vertical line), which cannot be represented in the other two forms. However, this form doesn't immediately show the slope.*
- *The slope-intercept form is a special case of the standard form where b is restricted to 1. This form helps us immediately identify the slope of the line (and the y-intercept). Also, it's the form used when we talk about linear functions.*

The point-slope form is also a special case of the standard form where b is restricted to 1. In addition, the point-slope form serves the purpose of clearly displaying a point on the graph of the equation and its slope. Finally, the point-slope form is, in principle, essentially the same as the slope-intercept form because the information given to figure out the equation is the same (i.e., in both cases, the slope is given, plus one point on the line: in the slope-intercept form the point given is $(0, b)$ where b is the y-intercept; in the point slope form the point given is (p, q). Note that, in the latter case, if p = 0, then (p, q) is the point where the line intersects the y-axis. Therefore, it can be used to write the linear equation in slope-intercept form. Likewise, given the y-intercept, we can write the linear equation in point-slope form. So all three forms of linear equation serve distinctive purposes.

Note the respondent helps students to connect the general forms of equations (i.e., using symbols) with the concrete examples they have worked on. Furthermore, instead of asking students to mindlessly memorize different forms of linear equations, the respondent emphasizes the connection between different forms and between the algebraic and geometric representations of linear equations. Throughout, we see the respondent is deliberate at using definition as a basis for logical reasoning, emphasizing and connecting key mathematical ideas, and scaffolding the reasoning process in a coherent way from simple to complex and from specific to general. Overall, the response is complete and characterized with precision, coherence, and purposefulness.

Quadratic Functions and Their Graphs

Quadratic functions are significantly more complex, mathematically, than linear functions. However, the key to helping students learn this topic is for students to have a firm grasp of the graph of the quadratic function and its algebraic expression. Several central mathematical ideas are behind the scenario questions (see 3.1 to 3.4 in Table 6.2) on a quadratic function and its graph, including, firstly to enable students to have comfort and familiarity with the graph of the quadratic function, through knowing the graph of the unit quadratic function $g(x) = x^2$. This foundational understanding sets students on the path to understanding (a) how standard quadratic functions $f_a(x) = ax^2$ relate to $g(x)$, which is that graphs of $f_a(x)$ are dilations of the graph of $g(x)$. Or put it differently, the graphs of $f_a(x)$ are similar to the graph of the unit quadratic function $g(x)$. In addition, it is important to help students understand, (b) that the graph of $f(x) = ax^2 + bx + c$ is congruent to the graph of some standard quadratic function $f_a(x) = ax^2$ through translation. And combined (i.e., items a and b), these two ideas help students understand that all the graphs of quadratic functions $f(x) = ax^2 + bx + c$ are similar to each other. Then secondly, to help students understand how to rewrite the standard form into the vertex and root forms, both graphically and algebraically (i.e., completing the square). And, thirdly, to help students understand why the vertex and root forms are better than the standard polynomial form that is typically given. In other words, what information about the graph does each of these forms (i.e., vertex and root forms) contain about the quadratic function that is not available in the standard form? How does the quadratic formula fit in all of this? And what do we know about the connection between the roots of the quadratic function (if the discriminant is greater than or equal to zero) and the constants? Let's see how these key ideas are scaffolded in the exemplary responses to the questions.

The graph of quadratic functions. Question 3.1 focuses on enabling students to have comfort and familiarity with the graph of the quadratic function, through knowing the graph of the unit quadratic function $g(x) = x^2$.

As shown in the following response, the respondent is purposeful and emphasizes the key ideas underlying the mathematical activities:

> *The key idea I hope students would understand is that the graph of $f(x) = ax^2 + bx + c$ is similar to the graph of $g(x) = x^2$ through dilation and translation (and reflection if $a < 0$). But how do we get there? What kind of translation will take us from the graph of $f_a(x) = ax^2$ to the graph of $f(x) = ax^2 + bx + c$ (after transforming the graph of $g(x)$ into the graph of $f_a(x)$ through dilation by scale factor of $\frac{1}{a}$ and centered at the origin)?*

In addition, the respondent is very deliberate at using definition as a basis for logical reasoning:

I'd first help students understand that, for a point to be on the graph of a function f(x) (whether linear or quadratic), it means that the x-coordinate and y-coordinate of the point are connected through the given function in the following way: (x,f(x)). Furthermore, the graph of a function f(x) is the collection of all points of the form (x,f(x)).

With this foundational understanding, the respondent shows a carefully thought-out guided practice to scaffold complex ideas through simple, concrete examples:

With this understanding, the first quadratic function we would consider is $g(x) = x^2$. To help students graph $g(x) = x^2$ by hand, I would have them set up a table with the following x-values:

x
–3
–2
–1
0
1
2
3

Then I would ask them: How do we find the points on the graph of g that have these x-values? I would expect students to recall the definition above and realize that they first need to calculate $g(x)$ for each of the x-values listed.

x	$g(x) = x^2$
–3	$g(-3) = (-3)^2 = 9$
–2	$g(-2) = (-2)^2 = 4$
–1	$g(-1) = (-1)^2 = 1$
0	$g(0) = (0)^2 = 0$
1	$g(1) = 1$
2	$g(2) = 4$
3	$g(3) = 9$

Then each point $(x,g(x))$ would be a point on the graph of g. Therefore, their graph of g would include the points (0, 0), (–1, 1), (1, 1), (2, 4), (–2, 4), (3, 9), (–3, 9).

Once the students are familiarized and feel comfortable with this simple quadratic function, the respondent pushes their thinking further, again through a concrete example:

Then I'd say, now let's look at how the graph changes when we change the coefficient of x^2 in the function $g(x) = x^2$. First of all, what is the coefficient of x^2 in the unit quadratic $g(x) = x^2$? [Answer = 1] That means, we want to look at graphs of $f_a(x) = ax^2$ where a is not 1 (or 0). Let's first consider the case when a is positive, say 2. What will the graph of $f_2(x) = 2x^2$ look like? I would expect students to suggest we use the same method as before and expand the table;

x	$g(x) = x^2$	$f_2(x) = 2x^2$
–3	$g(-3) = (-3)^2 = 9$	$f_2(-3) = 2(-3)^2 = 18$
–2	$g(-2) = (-2)^2 = 4$	etc.
–1	$g(-1) = (-1)^2 = 1$	
0	$g(0) = (0)^2 = 0$	
1	$g(1) = 1$	
2	$g(2) = 4$	
3	$g(3) = 9$	

Then we would consider when a is negative, say –2. Again, we would expand the table:

x	$g(x) = x^2$	$f_2(x) = 2x^2$	$f_{-2}(x) = -2x^2$
–3	$g(-3) = (-3)^2 = 9$	$f_2(-3) = 2(-3)^2 = 18$	$f_{-2}(-3) = -2(-3)^2 = -18$
–2	$g(-2) = (-2)^2 = 4$	etc.	etc.
–1	$g(-1) = (-1)^2 = 1$		
0	$g(0) = (0)^2 = 0$		
1	$g(1) = 1$		
2	$g(2) = 4$		
3	$g(3) = 9$		

As can be seen, the respondent is very deliberate in carefully scaffolding the complex ideas in a systematic and coherent way to the students. At the end of these activities, the respondent is very purposeful about bringing mathematical closure to the key concepts and ideas that students should acquire through these exercises:

After graphing $f_2(x) = 2x^2 f_{-2}(x) = -2x^2$ and a few more cases, I'd have a class discussion along the line of: What happens to the graph when the coefficient of x^2 changes? And by extension (or generalization), what does the coefficient "a" do to the graph of g to get to the graph of f_a? What happens when "a" is positive? What happens when "a" is negative? I would expect students to offer the following observations:

- *When a is positive and greater than 1, the graph appears to keep the same shape as the graph of g but looks "thinner" than the graph of g.*
- *When a is positive and between 0 and 1, the graph appears to keep the same shape as the graph of g but looks "wider" than the graph of g.*
- *When a is negative, the graph appears to be the reflection across the y-axis of the cases above.*

I would explain to students that describing the graph of f_a as the "same shape" but "thinner" or "wider" than the graph of g means the graph of f_a is similar to the graph of g. By definition of similarity, that means the graph of f_a is a dilation of the graph of g. I would have students confirm this fact with the following

exercise (assuming students have had ample practice with dilations before this): dilate the points of g found earlier by a scale factor $\frac{1}{2}$ and center at the origin

$(0,0)$. Students should find that the dilated points coincide with the points found earlier for the graph of f_2 and, therefore, this dilation transforms the graph of g to the graph of f_2.

Next, we see that the respondent extends students' thinking by pushing them to work with general forms (i.e., use symbols) following the same logic they used with concrete examples. The respondent is very deliberate at demonstrating the interconnectedness of mathematical ideas and showing the logical progression of mathematical ideas:

Following the same logic as outlined above (i.e., how I'd help students understand the connection between g and f_a when $a \neq 1$ or 0), I'd systematically ask students to graph the following functions, by hand:

- *$h_q(x) = ax^2 + q$*
  First, set $a = 2$ and vary q (e.g., let q be 1, 2, -1, -2). Next, set $a = -2$ and vary q in the same way. Then have a discussion on what "q" does to the graph: What happens when "q" is positive? What happens when "q" is negative? I would want students to conclude that the q translates the graph of f_a q units up when $q > 0$ and q units down when $q < 0$.

- $h(x) = a(x - p)^2 + q$
  In the same manner, I'd set $a = 2, q = 1$ but vary p and have students graph each case. Then, I'd have a discussion on what "p" does to the graph. I would want students to conclude that the p translates the graph of h p units to the left when $p < 0$ and p units to the right when $p > 0$.
- Key idea: the graph of h is the translation $T(x,y) = (x + p, y + q)$ of the graph of f_a (i.e., every point in the graph of f_a translates p units horizontally and q units vertically).

Finally, the respondent shows the purposefulness by emphasizing the key ideas and bringing mathematical closure to what students are doing:

Once students have graphed a few functions of the form $h(x) = a(x - p)^2 + q$, I'd ask students to compare how constants p, q might be related to the constants b, c if $h(x) = a(x - p)^2 + q$ is expanded to the form $f(x) = ax^2 + b + c$. The purpose is to help students see that all quadratic functions of the form $f(x) = ax^2 + b + c$ can be rewritten as $f(x) = a(x - p)^2 + q$. And the key to accomplish this is via the so-called "completing the squares."

Different forms of quadratic function. Question 3.2 (see Table 6.2) focuses on helping students understand how to rewrite the standard form into the vertex and root forms, both graphically and algebraically (i.e., completing the square).

As can be seen below, the respondent is purposeful about the key mathematical ideas that students need to understand:

The key mathematical ideas for this question are for students to understand that any quadratic function of the form $f(x) = ax^2 + b + c$ can be rewritten into: (1) the vertex form $a(x - h)^2 + k$ through the technique of completing the square; and (2) the root form $a(x - p)(x - q)$ if we know the root(s) of the quadratic function (and the roots are given by the quadratic formula, assuming discriminant $b^2 - 4ac \geq 0$).

In addition, the respondent demonstrates a deliberate effort at scaffolding ideas in a systematic and coherent way: showing the interconnectedness of ideas both geometrically and algebraically and scaffolding the reasoning from simple to complex and from specific to general. These features are well demonstrated in the following response:

So how would I go about accomplishing this teaching and learning goal?

(1)   *Standard form to vertex form:*

I would graphically show the logic of completing the square and then algebraically manipulate the standard form to vertex form. In other words, I would start with the diagram approach first. Once students understand what "completing the square" looks like graphically, I'd go over how we do the general case through algebraic manipulation.

Step 1: Graphically

Consider the expression $k^2 + l \cdot k$ where k, l are positive numbers. Then we can think of $k^2 + l \cdot k$ as $k^2 + \dfrac{l}{2} \cdot k + \dfrac{l}{2} \cdot k$, which is equal to the area of the square with side length k, plus the areas of two rectangles each with side lengths k and $\dfrac{l}{2}$, as shown below:

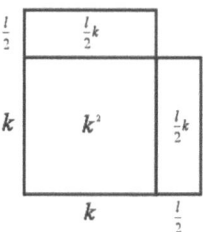

As the diagram shows, we could form a larger square with side length $k + \dfrac{l}{2}$ if we added in a square at the top right corner. What would be the area of such a square? $\left(\dfrac{l}{2}\right)^2$.

Then the area of this larger square is $\left(k + \dfrac{l}{2} \right)^2$. Therefore, if we add $\left(\dfrac{l}{2} \right)^2$ to

our original expression $k^2 + l \cdot k$, we "complete the square". Symbolically:

$$k^2 + l \cdot k + \left(\dfrac{l}{2} \right)^2 = \left(k + \dfrac{l}{2} \right)^2.$$

Step 2: Algebraically

I would start with concrete cases of $x^2 + bx$ (e.g., $x^2 + 8x, x^2 + 5x, x^2 - 6x, x^2 - \dfrac{3}{4}x$)

and ask students, what do we need to add to each of these expressions in order to be able to rewrite each one in the form $(x + ?)^2$? Building upon the graphical approach in Step 1, students should see the following pattern: $x^2 + bx + \left(\dfrac{b}{2} \right)^2 = \left(x + \dfrac{b}{2} \right)^2$. I would summarize their work on the concrete cases with this general case, which can be transformed into: $x^2 + bx = \left(x + \dfrac{b}{2} \right)^2 - \left(\dfrac{b}{2} \right)^2$.

Then I would do concrete cases of $x^2 + bx + c$ (e.g., $x^2 + 8x + 2$, $x^2 + 5x - 1, x^2 - \dfrac{3}{4}x - \dfrac{5}{64}$) and ask students, how can we rewrite each of the expressions in the form $(x + ?)^2$, plus some constant? Based on students' work, I would summarize with the general case:

$$x^2 + bx + c = \left(x + \dfrac{b}{2} \right)^2 + \left(c - \left(\dfrac{b}{2} \right) \right)^2$$

Finally, I would have concrete cases of $ax^2 + bx + c$ (e.g., $2x^2 + 8x - 5$) and ask students, how can we rewrite the expressions so that each one has $(x + ?)^2$ in it?

Finally, the respondent is purposeful in terms of bringing a mathematical closure to what students are learning, namely, converting a quadratic function from its standard form to vertex form:

Once they understand the concrete cases, I'd work with them through the general case in the function form:

$$f(x) = ax^2 + bx + c$$

$$= a\left(x^2 + \frac{b}{a}x\right) + c$$

$$= a\left(x^2 + \frac{b}{a}x + ?\right) + c + ??$$

I would ask students to determine what ? and ?? should be so that

$$f(x) = a(x + number)^2 + (another\ number)$$

Our conclusion would be $f(x) = ax^2 + bx + c = a\left(x + \frac{b}{2a}\right)^2 + c - \frac{b^2}{4a}$

I would then ask students, where have we seen quadratic functions that look like this? Hopefully they would recall the form a(x − h)² + k from work in question 1. Then, as a final exercise, I would have the students find the relationship between the constants, which would get the following: $h = -\frac{b}{2a},\ k = c - \frac{b^2}{4a}$.

When helping students to understand how to convert quadratic function from standard form to root form, the respondent is explicit about using definition as a basis for logical reasoning:

Step 1: Definitions of "zero of a quadratic function" and "root of a quadratic equation"

We define x_0 to be a zero of a quadratic function $f(x) = ax^2 + bx + c$ if $f(x_0) = 0$. We define r_0 to be a root of a quadratic equation $ax^2 + bx + c = 0$ if r_0 is a solution to the equation $ax^2 + bx + c = 0$. That means, a root of a quadratic equation $ax^2 + bx + c = 0$ is a zero of the quadratic function $f(x) = ax^2 + bx + c$ (and vice versa).

Using this definition, the respondent carefully scaffolds the ideas through a systematic and coherent progression by helping students understand: (1) the relationship between roots of a quadratic equation and x-intercepts of a quadratic function; (2) using this relationship to locate the x-intercepts of a quadratic function; and (3) transform the quadratic function from standard form to root form.

Why do we need different forms of quadratic functions? Questions 3.3 and 3.4 focus on different forms of quadratic functions. The primary purpose of these two scenario questions is to examine ways in which teachers help students to understand that each form of the quadratic function provides some information about the quadratic function and to see the connection between algebraic and geometric representations of quadratic function. An exemplary response again exhibits characteristics of coherence and purposefulness. For example, the following response shows a deliberate effort at showing the logical progression from using concrete examples to using general cases:

> *First, I'd ask students to graph a specific quadratic function, say$f(x) = 2x^2 + 8x + 5$. I would expect them to do this by, first, rewriting the function into the form $a(x - h)^2 + k$ as explained in question 2, and then, using the method outlined in question 1, they would translate the graph of $f_2(x) = 2x^2$ to get the graph of $f(x) = 2x^2 + 8x + 5$. Then I'd ask them to work in groups or pairs to figure out the following:*
>
>   1. *At what value(s) of x does the graph intersect the x-axis? What does it mean when the graph of the function intersects the x-axis?*
>   2. *Where is the line of symmetry? Draw it.*
>
> *At what value of x does the function achieve its maximum or minimum value? How do you know? When does a quadratic function have a maximum value? When does it have a minimum value?*

Not only that, the respondent connects mathematical ideas students are learning now with what they were doing previously:

> *The first set of questions relates back to question 2, (2). There we showed how to find the roots of the quadratic equation algebraically (and by connecting Step 2 of (1) and Step 3 of (2) we can get the quadratic formula, which is a quick and mechanical way to get the roots directly from the quadratic function in standard form, assuming the discriminant is greater than or equal to zero). We can also find the roots of the quadratic equation (which are the x-intercepts or zeros of the quadratic function) by using the graph: we see that the graph of $f(x) = a(x - h)^2 + k$ intersects the x-axis k units above the vertex (h, k). Because the graph of $f_a(x) = ax^2$ is congruent to the graph of f (as discussed in question 1), we can find the x-intercepts by finding the x-values when $f_a(x) = -k$. The result is $x = \pm\sqrt{\dfrac{-k}{a}}$, which means the x-intercepts of f are $\pm\sqrt{\dfrac{-k}{a}}$ from the axis of symmetry $x = h$ (see graph below).*

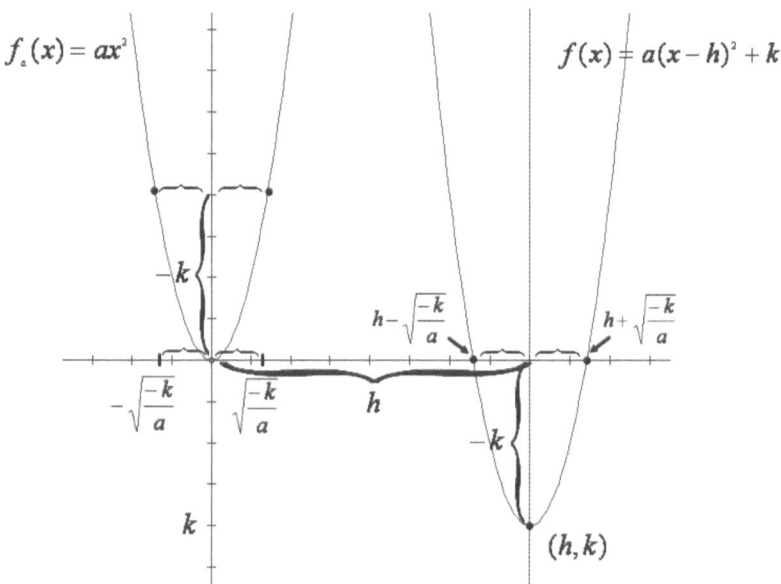

In addition to helping students connect mathematical ideas learned previously, the respondent is also deliberate at helping students to connect the algebraic and geometric representations:

> *By looking at the graph, students should also notice that the vertex is the point at which the function achieves its maximum (when the constant a < 0) or minimum value (when the constant a > 0). The vertex is (h, k) because, if a > 0 then $a(x - h)^2 \geq 0$ and thus $f \geq k$ so f achieves its minimum when $a(x - h)^2 = 0$, i.e, x = h. The argument is similar when a < 0.*

Finally, the respondent is purposeful at emphasizing key mathematical ideas in order to bring mathematical closure to the concepts that students are learning:

> *At the conclusion of the exercise, I would ask, so what is the value of writing the quadratic function in the form $f(x) = a(x - h)^2 + k$? I would expect students to say: it tells us the vertex, the axis of symmetry, and how to translate the graph of $f_a(x) = ax^2$ to the graph of f. I would then ask, so what is the value of the root form (which they learned to derive in Question 2)? I would expect students to say: it tells us the roots of the quadratic equation, which are the x-intercepts, as well as the zeros, of the quadratic function.*

In this way, students can see that the vertex form and root form provide them with all there is to know about the graph of a quadratic function. However, it's the standard form that immediately tells us the quadratic function is a member of the broader family of polynomial functions. Therefore, each form tells us something about the function but not everything (the vertex form doesn't immediately give us the roots, the root form doesn't immediately give us the vertex, the standard form doesn't tell us much about how the graph looks).

To summarize, this chapter describes what conceptual mathematical understandings of foundational arithmetic and algebra topics might look like and describes key attributes that characterize such understanding. As can be seen in the examples, conceptual mathematical understanding exemplifies precision, coherence, and purposefulness. There is consistent and substantial evidence of an attempt to emphasize the key mathematical idea, its rationale, the logical progression of mathematical concepts, and the connectedness among different mathematical concepts, procedures, and ideas. In addition, these responses pay deliberate attention to scaffolding mathematical ideas to students in a systematic and coherent way, from simple to complex and from specific to general.

This kind of content understanding that is foundational for building a coherent conceptual picture of K-12 mathematics was by no means commonplace or available in the mathematics (Wu 2011b, 2016a, b) or emphasized by the mathematics education literature until now (e.g., Newton and Poon 2015a, b). The fact that few seem to recognize how drastically different the Common Core Mathematics Standards are from pre-Common Core standards used by different states and the widespread misconception of what Common Core Mathematics Standards are and are not is a testimony of how cultural beliefs surrounding mathematics and its teaching will profoundly influence how reform efforts work themselves out in practice. It is no wonder that waves of K-12 mathematics education reforms have come and gone and yet we see little improvement in students' mathematics outcomes if we define the outcomes in terms of their ability to reason mathematically, to think critically, to see the mathematical coherence, and to have the capacity for transferring what they learn from one context to another (e.g., transferring what they learn about whole numbers to fractions and to algebra and so on). The concluding chapter (Chap. 7) will discuss these issues and place mathematics teachers' content training in the broader context in the USA.

References

Ball, D. L. (1990). The mathematical understanding that prospective teachers bring to teacher education. *Elementary School Journal, 90*, 449–466.

Ball, D. L., Hill, H. C., & Bass, H. (2005). Knowing mathematics for teaching: Who knows mathematics well enough to teach third grade, and how can we decide? *American Educator, 29*(3), 14.

Ball, D. L., Hoover, M. H., & Phelps, G. (2008). Content knowledge for teaching: What makes it special. *Journal of Teacher Education, 59*(5), 389–407.

Baumert, J., Kunter, M., Blum, W., Brunner, M., Voss, T., Jordan, A., & Klusmann, U. (2010). Teachers' mathematical knowledge, cognitive activation in the classroom, and student progress. *American Educational Research Journal, 47*(1), 133–180.

Gardner, H. (1991). *Unschooled mind: How children think and how schools should teach*. New York: Basic Books.

Gursky, D. (1991). The unschooled mind. *Education Week Teacher*. Retrieved http://www.edweek.org/tm/articles/1991/11/01/3gardner.h03.html

Ma, L. (1999). *Knowing and teaching elementary mathematics: Teachers' understanding of fundamental mathematics in China and the United States*. Mahwah: Lawrence Erlbaum Assoc.

Ma, L. (2010). *Knowing and teaching elementary mathematics: Teachers' understanding of fundamental mathematics in China and the United States* (2nd ed.). New York: Routledge.

Newton, X., & Poon, R. (2015a). Mathematical content understanding for teaching: A study of undergraduate STEM majors. *Creative Education, 6*(10), 998–1031. https://doi.org/10.4236/ce.2015.610101

Newton, X., & Poon, R. (2015b). Pre-service STEM majors' understanding of slope according to common Core mathematics standards: An exploratory study. *Global Journal of Human Social Science Research, 15*(7), 27–42.

Schoenfeld, A. H., & Kilpatrick, J. (2008). Toward a theory of proficiency in teaching mathematics. *International Handbook of Mathematics Teacher Education, 2*, 1–35.

Shulman, L. S. (1986). Those who understand: Knowledge growth in teaching. *Educational Researcher, 15*(2), 4–14.

Shulman, L. S. (1999). Forward. In L. Ma (Ed.), *Knowing and teaching elementary mathematics: Teachers' understanding of fundamental mathematics in China and the United States*. Mahwah: Lawrence Erlbaum Associates, Inc.

Skemp, R. R. (1976/2006). Relational understanding and instrumental understanding. *Mathematics Teaching in the Middle School, 12*(2), 88–95. Originally published in Mathematics Teaching.

Wu, H. S. (1998). Teaching fractions in elementary schools: A manual for teachers. Accessible at: https://math.berkeley.edu/~wu/fractions1998.pdf

Wu, H. S. (2002). *Chapter 2: Fractions (draft)*. Accessible at: https://math. berkeley.edu/~wu/EMI2a.pdf

Wu, H. (2006). How mathematicians can contribute to K-12 mathematics education. In Proceedings of International Congress of Mathematicians, 2006, Madrid, Volume III (1676–1688). Zürich, Switzerland: European Mathematical Society. http://math.berkeley.edu/~wu/ICMtalk.pdf

Wu, H. S. (2010). *The mathematics teachers should know*. Talk given at Lisbon, Portugal, on January 29, 2010. Accessible at: http://math.berkeley.edu/~wu/ Lisbon2010_2.pdf

Wu, H. S. (2011a). The miss-education of mathematics teachers. *Notices of the American Mathematical Society, 58*(3), 372–384.

Wu, H. S. (2011b). *Understanding numbers in elementary school mathematics*. Providence: American Mathematical Society.

Wu, H. S. (2011c). *The mathematics early grade teachers need to know| and what it means to know it*. Talk given at Rio de Janeiro. Accessible at: https://math. berkeley.edu/~wu/Brazil2.pdf

Wu, H. (2014). Textbook School Mathematics and the preparation of mathematics teachers. Accessible at: https://math.berkeley.edu/~wu/Stony_Brook_2014. pdf

Wu, H. S. (2016a). *Teaching school mathematics: Pre-algebra*. Providence: American Mathematical Society.

Wu, H. S. (2016b). *Teaching school mathematics: Algebra*. Providence: American Mathematical Society.

CHAPTER 7

Placing Mathematics Teachers' Content Training in the Broader Context in the USA

This chapter focuses on several contextual factors that shape teachers' and students' opportunities to learn mathematics and contextualizes how mathematics practices function within the broader system in the USA. This contextualization will promote deeper understanding of the reasons why K-12 mathematics practices work the way they do and heighten the need for higher education institutions to step up and offer future mathematics teachers the proper mathematics courses needed for teaching K-12 students. Such an understanding is critical as policy makers consider launching the next wave of mathematics reform (e.g., the Common Core Mathematics Standards) or importing practices that appear successful in other countries (e.g., Japanese lesson studies, Singapore mathematics, Chinese Shanghai mathematics, Finish education, and so on).

This chapter is important because what we observe in classroom teaching and learning and what we see in students' performance against various accountability measures such as high-stakes, large-scale, standardized tests are products of many things. Among these many things are ways how teachers themselves learned the subject matter, how they were trained to be teachers during their credentialing process, and how they were trained and supported once they entered the teaching force. Above all, teaching and learning and the education policies that drive them at their core are cultural activities that are highly complex, because what we observe in how schools carry out their daily business is really a reflection of the underlying philosophical and epistemological conceptions of what teaching and learning are about.

© The Author(s) 2018   181
X. A. Newton, *Improving Teacher Knowledge in K-12 Schooling*,
https://doi.org/10.1007/978-3-319-71207-9_7

Consequently, in presenting observations of the way that teachers engage their students about mathematics, the way that teachers use various kinds of instructional tools and resources that are provided to them, and the impact of such tools upon classroom mathematics teaching and learning, we also want to be attentive to some of the broader contextual issues in order to put the findings in a proper perspective.

Among these contextual factors are the US cultural perspectives on mathematics teaching and learning, the US K-12 school system and the challenges involved in changing core practice, and the impact of the accountability system such as the No Child Left Behind (NCLB) Act and other similar Acts (e.g., the Every Student Succeeds Act). These contextual factors to a great extent provide an insight into understanding the challenges involved in improving the teaching and learning conditions for K-12 mathematics, challenges that are not unique to any mathematics reform efforts (e.g., new mathematics, common core mathematics, and so on). Such an insight heightens the need for higher education institutions to step up and offer future mathematics teachers the proper mathematics courses needed for teaching K-12 students.

US Cultural Perspectives on Mathematics Teaching and Learning

Building on Cuban's (1993) view of the role of cultural beliefs, Chazan (2000) has suggested that the widespread and deeply rooted cultural beliefs about the nature of knowledge, how teaching should occur, and how children should learn has a special flavor when we focus on mathematics instruction. According to Chazan, in western views of knowledge, mathematics is often described as the most certain branch of human knowledge. In mathematics, it is easy to distinguish "right" from "wrong." The notions central to this set of beliefs about mathematics instruction are that:

- All statements of school mathematics can be judged unequivocally right or wrong.
- A central role of the teacher is to exercise this judgment.
- These judgments can be used effectively to label students' "ability" or aptitude in mathematics. (p. 115)

Because of these beliefs, Chazan argued that teachers have difficulty in creating authentic conversations with students about mathematics. Naturally, if teachers know what is right or wrong, what is there to discuss? Therefore, in typical teacher-centered classrooms, a large chunk of instructional time is devoted to teacher lecture. Students ask clarifying questions. If there is any confusion on the students' part, this is regarded as problematic and therefore further explanation or practice is required without a diagnosis of why students do not understand the materials.

Besides a heavy emphasis on truth and correctness, it is a common practice in the USA to give much weight to ability, unlike other societies that may emphasize effort rather than ability (Stevenson and Stigler 1992; Stigler and Hiebert 1999; Stigler et al. 1990). On top of all this, it is widely accepted in the USA that elementary mathematics is basic, superficial, commonly understood, and repetitive (Ma 1999, 2010). Therefore, starting from the stage of building foundational skills, students are not taught or given the opportunities to reason mathematically, to communicate about mathematical ideas, and make connections among mathematical ideas and between mathematics and their own daily lives. However, when they do not do well on tests, they are labeled as "low ability" and are therefore held back and considered as problematic (e.g., lack of maturity to learn the topics, lack of motivation, disciplinary behaviors, and so on).

However, Chazan showed through his own teaching of mathematics (Algebra) to lower-track secondary students that the notion of ability was problematic, because: (1) when students accept this label (i.e., low ability), they have a ready-made explanation for expecting that tasks posed for them are too difficult to attempt, whereas if teachers accept this label, their energies and efforts at understanding the students are undercut; and (2) the impact of the notion of ability on classroom dynamics in less advanced track classrooms can be twofold. If students are so used to being judged as "low ability," they are afraid to share their thinking because they are concerned that once again they may be evaluated to show how little they know. If, on the other hand, students have all done poorly in mathematics, why should they listen to each other?

These two dynamics in classrooms involving less advanced students make it particularly challenging for teachers who desire to make mathematics teaching and learning meaningful.

US K-12 SCHOOL SYSTEM: CHANGING THE CORE
OF EDUCATIONAL PRACTICE

In his study on "Getting Scale with Good Educational Practice,", Richard Elmore (1996) pointed out several challenges involved in fundamentally improving "the core of educational practice," which are thought-provoking and insightful. The sections that follow provide an overview of his points and then relate them to some of the issues that are relevant to reform efforts at fundamentally changing mathematics teaching and learning.

Elmore (1996) defined "the core of educational practice" as "how teachers understand the nature of knowledge and the student-teacher role in learning, and how these ideas about knowledge and learning are manifested in teaching and class work." According to Elmore and some other researchers (e.g., Cohen 1990), most teachers tend to think of knowledge as discrete bits of information about a particular subject and of student learning as the acquisition of this information through processes of repetition, memorization, and regular testing of recall. The teacher, who is generally the center of attention in the classroom, initiates most of the talk and orchestrates most of the interaction in the classroom around brief factual questions, if there is any discussion at all.

Their findings suggest that attempts to change such stable patterns of the core of schooling in any fundamental way are usually unsuccessful on anything more than a small scale. Schools, therefore, might be "changing" all the time (e.g., adopting this or that new structure or schedule or textbook series or tracking system), but never change in any fundamental way what teachers and students actually do when they are together in classrooms. In particular, the closer an innovation gets to the core of schooling, the less likely it is that it will influence teaching and learning on a large scale.

The problem of scale is not a problem of the general resistance or failure of schools to change. Most schools are, in fact, constantly changing, such as adopting new curricula, tests, and grouping practices, changing schedules, creating new mechanisms for participation in decision making, adding or subtracting teaching and administrative roles, and myriad other modifications. Within this vortex of change, however, basic conceptions of knowledge, of the teacher's and the student's role in constructing knowledge, and of the role of classroom and school level structures in enabling student learning remain relatively static.

This failure is rooted not only in the design of the institutions, but also in a deep cultural norm about teaching that successful teaching is an individual trait rather than a set of learned professional competencies acquired over the course of a career (Elmore 1996). It is not surprising, then, to observe that teaching has been characterized as an "isolated" practice which is not prone to outside influence.

Chapter 5's examination of the issues surrounding the key curricular tools and instructional resources echoes some of the issues that Elmore observed in his and other researchers' studies. For instance, when asked what changes can be made to the Math Instructional Guide (MIG) that would make it more useful as a guide, teachers indicated that it was difficult not having the standards aligned within a given quarter to the textbook. In addition, the need to "jump around" to find the sequential concept or skill in the textbook in order to teach the standards outlined within a quarter by the MIG was indeed unsatisfactory.

Although alternative materials have been introduced in the curriculum, many teachers still use the textbook as their primary teaching tool. Teaching mathematics is often defined as starting with chapter one and concluding with the last chapter. In other words, there is a comfort level using the text from beginning to end in sequential and chronological order. Consequently, teachers have difficulty and dislike having to skip around the book.

Likewise, one of the biggest concerns for mathematics coaches and administrators in regards to the MIG is the organization of the standards in each quarter. Many feel frustrated, or they know their teachers are frustrated, with how the standards for each quarter are not aligned with the textbook or even sometimes the assessment test. They understand that teachers are used to following the textbook chronologically from beginning to end and have difficulty adjusting to skipping around the book. Although the leadership says they want teachers to focus more on the concepts that the standards encompass, rather than the textbook, teachers still see the textbook as their main resource and what should guide their curriculum.

Teachers' reliance on textbooks, worksheets, and homework was standard practice since the early twentieth century (Cuban 1993). Learning a new mathematics, therefore, is much more formidable for teachers than for students (Cohen 1990), because teachers must unlearn the mathematics and teaching practices that they have used for decades.

The Accountability Bottom Line: Higher Test Scores on High Stakes Tests

The reauthorization of the Elementary and Secondary Education Act (ESEA) first as the No Child Left Behind (NCLB) Act under the Bush administration and later as the Every Student Succeeds Act under the Obama administration have created an unprecedented demand on local states to mandate statewide testing of K-12 students in core subject areas and require that schools show Adequate Yearly Progress (AYP). Against this national context, Chap. 5 shows a district's math reform initiative as an orchestrated effort to align key instructional tools such as the MIG and periodic assessments with the state mathematics standards tests.

Data in Chap. 5, in particular, indicated that the use of the MIG and periodic assessments by teachers is only symptomatic of the larger climate, that is, one driven by the test. Though effort to rewrite the MIG has a focus on prioritizing and chunking standards, as well as helping teachers see the "big ideas" of mathematics for each quarter, it seems that what is termed as essential and must-know standards is heavily driven by what the state standard tests assess. Furthermore, the intended use of the mathematics periodic assessments (i.e., to use the assessment results for the purpose of improving instruction) is fairly limited. The district mathematics leadership team regarded "the best thing" about having on-going district-wide periodic assessments is that at least "all the topics are covered" or the assessments "force elementary teachers to teach math."

From the perspective of opportunities to learn, it is legitimate that students are taught and exposed to what they are going to be tested on. However, equating teaching and learning with preparations for high stakes tests and putting a singular emphasis on test scores demonstrate a narrow conception of teaching and learning, which works against the goal of fundamentally improving the quality of students' mathematics outcomes. This point becomes salient as we observe how the newest wave of mathematics reform, the adoption of the Common Core Mathematics Standards, was rolled out and backfired from its reliance on computerized standardized tests as the first step towards implementing the Common Core State Standards Initiative.

Common Core Mathematics Standards: A Good Effort That Is Going Awry

Common Core Mathematics Standards is part of the Common Core State Standards Initiative that delineates what students in K-12 should know in English Language, Arts and Mathematics at each grade level. The Initiative was sponsored by the National Governors Association (NGA) and the Council of Chief State School Officers (CCSSO) with the intention of ensuring that students are college ready or workforce ready. Unfortunately, for a variety of reasons, the Initiative has become increasingly political and whether the standards will have an impact on mathematics teaching and learning has yet to be seen. A thorough analysis of what went awry is beyond the scope of this book. However, data presented in Chap. 5 documenting a large school district's effort at transforming classroom mathematics teaching and learning could shed light on what might have gone wrong from the start.

Common Core Mathematics Standards represent a major departure from most pre-Common state standards, because Common Core emphasizes the logical sequence of mathematical topics and the connections among different mathematical ideas. Analysis done by Carmichael and colleagues (2010) shows that Common Core mathematics standards are superior to the mathematics standards of 39 states before Common Core. William Schmidt (2012) further commented:

> In my view, the Common Core State Standards in Mathematics (CCSSM) unquestionably represent a major change in the way U.S. schools teach mathematics. Rather than a fragmented system in which content is "a mile wide and an inch deep," the new common standards offer the kind of mathematics instruction we see in the top-achieving nations, where students learn to master a few topics each year before moving on to more advanced mathematics. It is my opinion that [a state] will best position its students for success by remaining committed to the Common Core State Standards and focusing their efforts on the implementation of the standards and aligned assessments.

Interestingly, while praising Common Core, Schmidt's comment also points to the problem of its implementation (i.e., "aligned assessments").

The implementation of Common Core seems to have put too much emphasis on the assessments from the start. Issues such as whether teachers are empowered to teach mathematical content at the level of rigor that

Common Core standards demand did not and still do not seem to get much attention. In addition, missing from the public discourse on Common Core mathematics standards are critical questions about who is writing the new curricular materials such as K-12 math textbooks, or who is providing educators (classroom teachers, mathematics coaches, etc.) with opportunities to learn content in a way that differs from what they learned as K-12 students (e.g., see Chap. 4's discussion on the concept of slope).

Not surprisingly, when New York state published the first wave of students' assessment results on common-core aligned tests, we saw headlines such as "Test Scores Sink as New York Adopts Tougher Benchmarks." Few seem to recognize the fact that Common Core mathematics content standards are asking for a fundamental shift in how content is conceptualized. Ralph Tyler (1991) wisely observed decades ago that teachers and students need time and opportunities to develop new understanding and skills when a new program differs in these respects from the old program. In the case of the Common Core mathematics standards, teachers are asked to teach and students are demanded to learn mathematics that is not familiar to what they are used to. Nonetheless, they are immediately held accountable for the Common Core assessment results without receiving a sustained and adequate training, or being provided with a set of curricular materials that are genuinely aligned with the new Common Core Mathematics Standards (Wu 2011c).

LEARNING FROM THE PAST AND GETTING TO THE ROOT CAUSE

This book's central argument is that teachers will need opportunities to be engaged in explicit, systematic, and rigorous content training of topics that they are charged to teach. As of now, there are three critical stages where teachers in the USA learn and acquire mathematical knowledge. These three critical stages include: (1) as K-12 students themselves, (2) as undergraduates in college and sometimes as teacher candidates if their teacher preparation programs require them to take more mathematics courses, and (3) as K-12 classroom teachers.

Because college mathematics (i.e., the content most teachers learned before becoming teachers) has little use in the K-12 classroom, K-12 mathematics textbooks become the primary source of subject matter knowledge for teachers. The problems with K-12 mathematics textbooks have been well documented (The National Mathematics Advisory Panel 2008) and Wu (2011a, c) labels such knowledge rooted in K-12 textbooks as Textbook School Mathematics (TSM).

This book shows how TSM manifests itself in K-12 classroom teaching and learning, in the kinds of professional development opportunities that teachers have as practicing teachers, and among undergraduate STEM majors who arguably represent the strongest pool of teacher candidates with strong content knowledge. To remedy the insufficient content preparation of mathematics teachers, the book argues that teachers will need opportunities to be engaged in explicit, systematic, and rigorous content training of topics that they are charged to teach.

These learning opportunities can come from pre-service specially designed mathematics courses and from in-service professional development activities. Fundamentally shifting in-service professional development practices is complex and beyond the scope of this book (see Newton 2007 for a detailed discussion on the institutional design of the US K-12 school systems versus the reform expectations). Higher education institutions could play an important role in breaking the cycle of poor learning experiences, inadequate foundational knowledge and skills for teaching, and weak educational outcomes in mathematics. Higher education institutions are where future mathematics teachers gain disciplinary knowledge and pedagogical skills necessary for them to function effectively as classroom teachers.

Fortunately, we can now build on the work of Wu who has written a series of textbooks that provides a systematic exposition of K-12 mathematics topics, published by the American Mathematical Society (Wu 2011b, 2016a, b). These textbooks present K-12 mathematical content that is both useable (or teachable) in K-12 classrooms and are respectful of the mathematical integrity (i.e., two critical criteria for developing mathematical conceptual understanding).

We need higher education institutions to step up their role in the proper content training of future mathematics teachers. Towards this end, I would like to end the book with a quote by Lee Shulman (1999). Shulman, a highly regarded teacher educator and scholar who proposed the concept of pedagogical content knowledge (1986), insisted almost 20 years ago that:

[t]he only place to break the vicious cycle that limits the mathematical knowledge of U.S. teachers is in the development of far more effective mathematics courses in U.S. undergraduate programs. But current undergraduate mathematics programs seem to have no place for teaching fundamental mathematics for understanding. If anything, such knowledge is misconstrued as remedial instead of recognizing that it is rigorous and deserving of university-level instruction. Mathematics departments must take responsibility for serving this national priority for both future teachers and future citizens. (p. xii)

REFERENCES

Carmichael, S. B., Martino, G., Porter-Magee, K., & Wilson, W. S. (2010). *The state of state standards – And the Common Core – In 2010*. Washington, DC: Thomas B. Fordham Institute.

Chazan, D. (2000). *Beyond formulas in mathematics and teaching: Dynamics of the high school Algebra classroom*. New York: Teachers College Press.

Cohen, D. (1990). A revolution in one classroom: The case of Mrs. Oublier. *Educational Evaluation and Policy Analysis, 12*(3), 311–329.

Cuban, L. (1993). *How teachers taught: Constancy and change in American classrooms, 1890–1990*. New York: Teachers College Press.

Elmore, R. (1996). Getting to scale with good educational practice. *Harvard Educational Review, 66*(1), 1–26.

Ma, L. (1999). *Knowing and teaching elementary mathematics: Teachers' understanding of fundamental mathematics in China and the United States*. Mahwah: Lawrence Erlbaum Associates.

Ma, L. (2010). *Knowing and teaching elementary mathematics: Teachers' understanding of fundamental mathematics in China and the United States* (2nd ed.). New York: Routledge.

National Mathematics Advisory Panel. (2008). *Reports of the task groups and subcommittees: Chapter 3: Report of the task group on conceptual knowledge and skills*. Washington, DC: U.S. Department of Education.

Newton, X. (2007). Reflections on the U.S. math reforms from a cross-national perspective. *Phi Delta Kappan, 88*(9), 681–685.

Schmidt, W. (2012 November 5). The common core state standards in Mathematics "The Common Core State Standards in Mathematics". *The Huffington Post*.

Shulman, L. S. (1986). Those who understand: Knowledge growth in teaching. *Educational Researcher, 15*(2), 4–14.

Shulman, L. S. (1999). Preface. In L. Ma (Ed.), *Knowing and teaching elementary mathematics: Teachers' understanding of fundamental mathematics in China and the United States*. Mahwah: Lawrence Erlbaum Associates Publishers.

Stevenson, H., & Stigler, J. (1992). *The learning gap: Why our schools are failing and what we can learn from Japanese and Chinese education.* New York: Summit Books, Simon & Schuster Inc.

Stigler, J., & Hiebert, J. (1999). *The teaching gap: Best ideas from the world's teachers for improving education in the classroom.* New York: The Free Press.

Stigler, J., Lee, S., & Stevenson, H. (1990). *Mathematical knowledge of Japanese, Chinese, and American elementary school children.* Reston: The National Council of Teachers of Mathematics.

Tyler, R. (1991). General statement on program evaluation. In M. W. McLaughlin & D. C. Phillips (Eds.), *Evaluation and education at quarter century: Ninetieth yearbook of the national society for the study of education* (pp. 3–17). Chicago: University of Chicago Press.

Wu, H. S. (2011a). The miss-education of mathematics teachers. *Notices of the American Mathematical Society, 58*(3), 372–384.

Wu, H. S. (2011b). *Understanding numbers in elementary school mathematics.* Providence: American Mathematical Society.

Wu, H. S. (2011c). Phoenix rising. Bringing the common core state mathematics standards to life. *American Educator, 35*(3), 3–13. Accessible at: http://www.aft.org/pdfs/americaneducator/fall2011/Wu.pdf

Wu, H. S. (2016a). *Teaching school mathematics: Pre-algebra.* Providence: American Mathematical Society.

Wu, H. S. (2016b). *Teaching school mathematics: Algebra.* Providence: American Mathematical Society.

Appendix: Study Background

This book is based on my research directing a five-year longitudinal evaluation of a mathematics reform initiative in one of the largest urban school districts in the USA and serving as a faculty advisor for the research and evaluation of an undergraduate experimental mathematics and science teacher preparation program in one of the research universities on the west coast of the USA.

For the longitudinal district evaluation, the sampling procedure used to select the original sample proceeded in two stages. First stage selection consisted of probabilities proportional to size selection of schools based on school enrollment. A total of 40 schools were selected in this manner from separate strata defined by schooling level: 20 elementary schools, 10 middle schools, and 10 high schools. At stage two, we randomly selected a constant number of teachers at specific grade levels within each school: two 2nd and two 4th grade teachers in each elementary school, four 8th grade teachers in each middle school, and four 10th grade teachers in each high school. A 10th grade math teacher was defined as having more than 50% 10th grade students enrolled. This resulted in 160 teachers (or classrooms). To the extent possible, the same teachers were followed over the entire five years. If a teacher left the school, we randomly selected a replacement teacher to observe. By the end of the fifth year, 52 of the initial 80 elementary teachers and 43 of the initial 80 secondary math teachers remained in the study. Over the course of the five years, a total of

© The Author(s) 2018
X. A. Newton, *Improving Teacher Knowledge in K-12 Schooling*,
https://doi.org/10.1007/978-3-319-71207-9

34 additional elementary and 49 additional secondary math teachers were included in the study because of the sample attrition. This gives a total of 114 elementary and 129 secondary math teachers respectively who were part of the study over the five years.

The slope study is based on a broader study of pre-service STEM teachers' content understanding of three foundational algebra topics at a west coast research university. Thirty-two (32) study participants were recruited from undergraduate courses that focus on K-12 mathematics and on mathematics teaching and learning. Of these 32 study participants, five (16%) were science majors, four (13%) were engineering majors, 16 (50%) were mathematics majors, and seven (22%) were humanities majors.

INDEX